CW00394957

EX · LIBRIS
Gabriel N Cherish

The 60s
A Very Peculiar History™

With added flower power

'To the detriment of almost every other group in society, the young and the beautiful picked up the 1960s and took the decade home as a toy.'

Roger Hutchinson, *High Sixties*, 1992

For Dave Marl,

Sixties survivor and kindred spirit

DA

Editor: Stephen Haynes
Editorial assistants: Rob Walker, Mark Williams

Published in Great Britain in MMXII by
Book House, an imprint of
The Salariya Book Company Ltd
25 Marlborough Place, Brighton BN1 1UB
www.salariya.com
www.book-house.co.uk

HB ISBN-13: 978-1-908177-92-6

1 3 5 7 9 8 6 4 2
A CIP catalogue record for this book is available from the British Library.
Printed and bound in Dubai.
Printed on paper from sustainable sources.

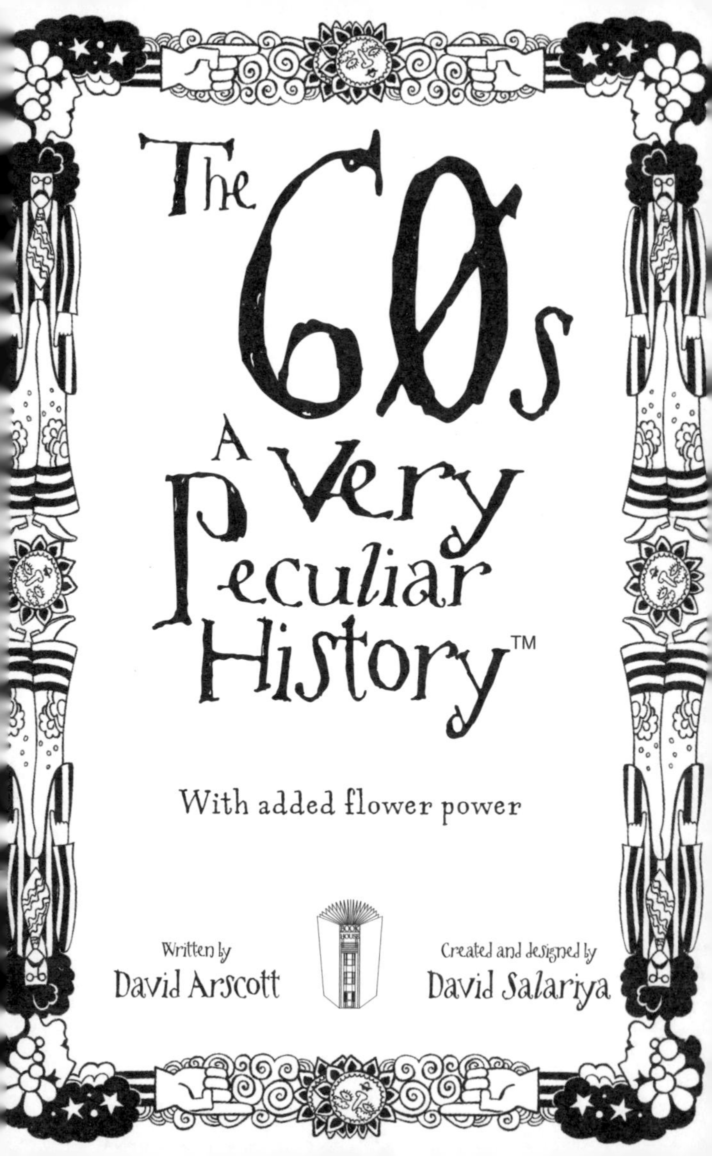

The 60s A Very Peculiar History™

With added flower power

Written by
David Arscott

Created and designed by
David Salariya

BOOK HOUSE

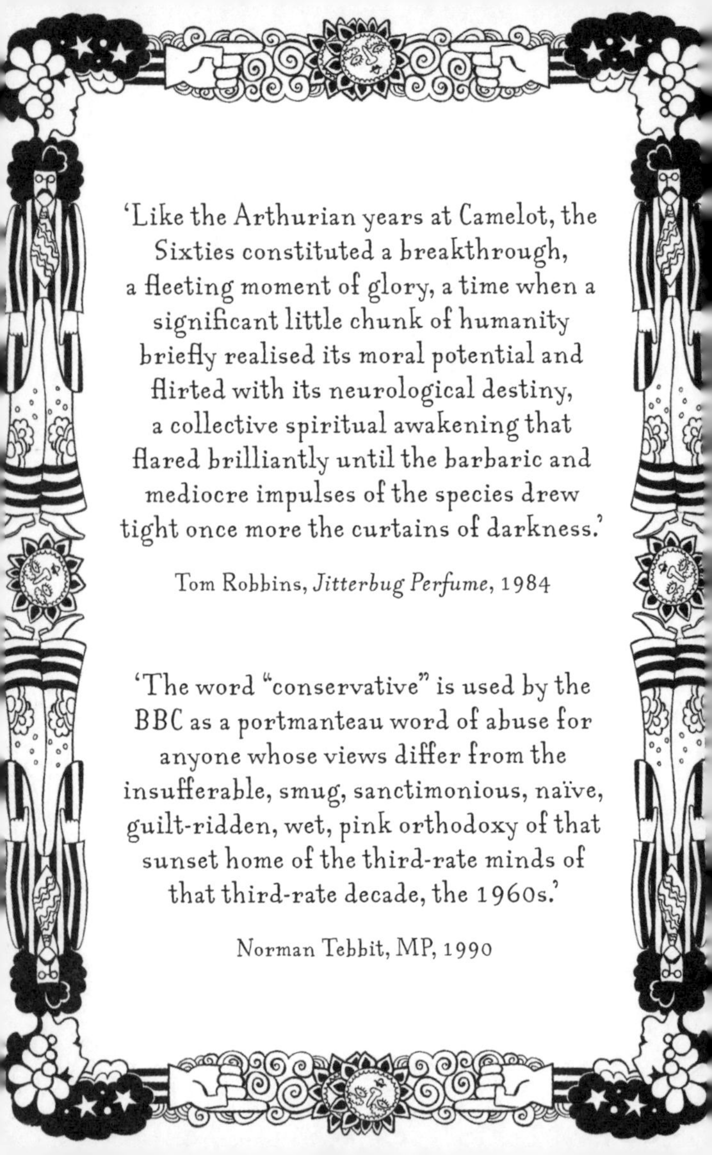

'Like the Arthurian years at Camelot, the Sixties constituted a breakthrough, a fleeting moment of glory, a time when a significant little chunk of humanity briefly realised its moral potential and flirted with its neurological destiny, a collective spiritual awakening that flared brilliantly until the barbaric and mediocre impulses of the species drew tight once more the curtains of darkness.'

Tom Robbins, *Jitterbug Perfume*, 1984

'The word "conservative" is used by the BBC as a portmanteau word of abuse for anyone whose views differ from the insufferable, smug, sanctimonious, naïve, guilt-ridden, wet, pink orthodoxy of that sunset home of the third-rate minds of that third-rate decade, the 1960s.'

Norman Tebbit, MP, 1990

Contents

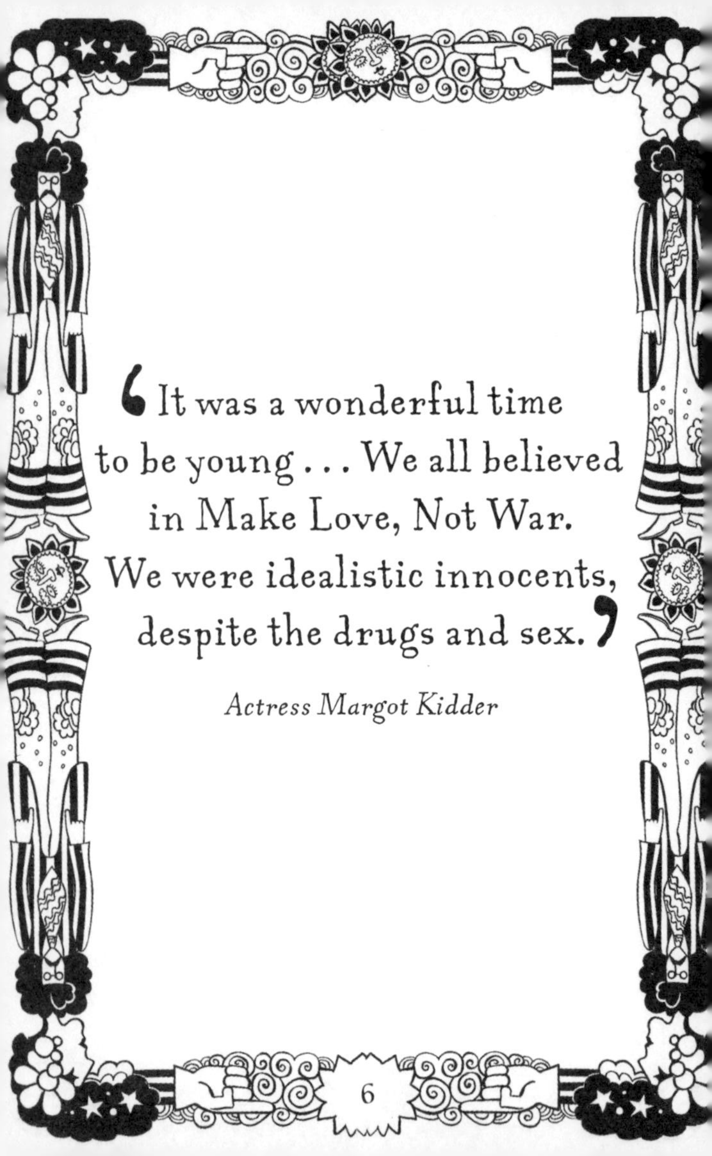

‘It was a wonderful time to be young . . . We all believed in Make Love, Not War. We were idealistic innocents, despite the drugs and sex.’

Actress Margot Kidder

OUT OF THE DARKNESS

It seems impossible to be neutral about the Sixties. The quotations on page 4 draw the battle lines: either it was a time of fruitful liberation, promising a flowering of love, equality, creativity and untrammelled self-expression, or it was a wretchedly irresponsible period, its legacy a breakdown of respect and decency, its damaging moral and social consequences still in evidence half a century later.

Although we'll surely agree that both positions are extreme, it's only fair to the reader to come clean at the outset: this book is largely a celebration of those gloriously giddy years.

The excuse, should one be needed, is my age. I was born in late 1942, and so had just turned 17 when the Sixties arrived. How could a teenager emerging from postwar British drabness fail to be stimulated by the heady promise – political, cultural, economic – of what was clearly a radiant new dawn?

The weary fifties

The story has to begin in the Fifties, both in order to make sense of the sheer exuberance of what was to follow and to acknowledge that the seeds of the coming revolution had already begun to sprout.

Our parents' generation (pathetically conformist, as we thought) had been battered first by the Depression and then by the Second World War. Ordinary people who had survived that conflict, whether fighting abroad or coping with enemy bombardment at home, had shown the spirit to choose a postwar government dedicated to a more egalitarian way of life – the National Health Service and all that. But those early fires had already dimmed by the beginning of the following decade when the old war leader Winston Churchill was voted back into 10 Downing Street.

Most families had little spare cash, meat rationing wasn't lifted in the UK until 1954, and those who had a decent job saw no reason to rock the boat by agitating for more pay. Enough was enough.

Many things were in short supply during the early 1950s:

- **Fridges:** Only about 15 per cent of homes had one.
- **Telephones:** Even fewer – and many shared a line with a neighbour.
- **Washing machines:** Most women (that's the way it was!) had to do it by hand.
- **Televisions:** Ownership was growing, but there was only one channel.
- **Central heating:** Not since the Romans left.

As for the physical landscape, that matched the general mood. In London and other cities hammered by the Luftwaffe there were large, undeveloped bombsites sprouting weeds.

After all, the country was still paying off its war debt to the Americans (and would continue to do so until as late as 2006).

More than a million unimaginatively designed council houses were thrown up to combat postwar homelessness, many of them in a rash of 'new towns' throughout the country. There were also some 150,000 'prefabs' – I was brought up in one myself – designed to last for ten years, but often surviving for much longer.

You never had it so good!

By the mid-1950s an economic recovery was on the way, and Prime Minister Harold Macmillan famously told a gathering of his Conservative supporters in July 1957 that 'Most of our people have never had it so good.'

He told his audience: 'Go around the country, go to the industrial towns, go to the farms and you will see a state of prosperity such as we have never had in my lifetime – nor indeed in the history of this country.'

He was right, but Britain wasn't yet a consumer society, and many felt that his boast was in pretty poor taste.

The American dream

This general dreariness was to give way, as the decade lengthened, to an economic boom – and anyone anxious to predict what this would mean for British society in the years ahead only had to look across the Atlantic to the already prosperous USA.

During the war gum-chewing GIs had been described as 'overpaid, oversexed and over here'. The Americans were back home now, but the exportable elements of their brash and confident culture cast a spell on many an aspirational inhabitant of this monochrome, tired little island, and especially on the young.

American films were much more lavish than anything made in the UK, and stars such as Marlon Brando and James Dean made the rebellious misfit an attractive role model in a society deadened by Cold War conformity.

fings weren't wot they used t'be!

At the very end of the 1950s Lionel Bart wrote the music and Cockney lyrics for Frank Norman's West End success *Fings Ain't Wot They Used t'Be*, directed by Joan Littlewood. The words of the title number list several contemporary social changes – and point the way forward to the Sixties...

> They changed our local Palais
> Into a bowling alley.

The British had always had their skittles, but the bowling alley was a craze straight from America.

> There used to be trams,
> Not very quick,
> Gotcha from place to place,
> But now there's just jams
> 'Alf a mile fick.

Car ownership had begun to spread, using roads ill prepared for the volume of traffic. The new towns had been designed with narrow streets, allowing just enough room for two cars to pass, since nobody had envisaged working-class families ever being able to afford their own transport.

> They stuck parking meters
> Outside our door to greet us.

Bart was up to the minute, because the very first of them had been installed (in Mayfair, London) on 10 July 1958.

Once our beer was frothy,
But now it's frothy coffee.

Tea had always been the national drink, but coffee bars were springing up the length and breadth of the land.

It used to be fun,
Dad an' old Mum
Paddling down Southend.

The English seaside holiday wasn't yet a last resort, but money in the pocket now allowed travel to hitherto unknown parts, and 'Paris is where we spend our outin's.'

Grandma tries to shock us all,
Doing knees-up rock and roll.

The 'big bands' were still in business, playing for a clientèle which enjoyed dancing the waltz and quickstep, but the raucous new music had already thoroughly seduced the young.

They're buying guitars, plinketty plonk,
Backing theirselves wiv free [3] chords only.

A skiffle group had a washboard and a tea-chest bass and a rock group had its drums, but the guitar was the ubiquitous instrument of the new music, however badly played.

Rock and *roll*

Where on earth, our parents asked, was the melody in the music we tuned in to on Radio Luxembourg every evening? There *were* melodies, of course, but what older folk recoiled from was its combination of aggressive rhythms and sexual explicitness.

Although there was still a place for crooners such as Frank Sinatra, Andy Williams and Perry Como, for the likes of Gracie Fields and the Beverley Sisters, and even for comedy numbers such as 'Seven Little Girls Sitting in the Back Seat, Kissing and a-Hugging with Fred', it was the rockers who were the coming force.

Elvis Presley recorded 'Heartbreak Hotel' in 1955 and had a string of hits before the end of the decade. Chuck Berry, Little Richard, Fats Domino and Buddy Holly were already household names (among the young), while Jerry Lee Lewis added scandal to the mix when he arrived in Britain newly married to his 13-year-old cousin. He had to fly back after only three concerts, tail between his legs.

The BBC bravely (and briefly) moved with the times by creating *The Six-Five Special,* a Saturday-evening programme devoted to popular music. The moody rock-and-rollers, often picked out dramatically from pitch darkness by a spotlight, included home-grown talent such as Marty Wilde, Vince Eager and Billy Fury – given their singing names by the rock impresario Larry Parnes.

The music's anarchic nature seemed to be exemplified by outbreaks of violence when *The Blackboard Jungle,* featuring Bill Hayley and the Comets' 'Rock Around the Clock', was screened in British cinemas in 1956.

The Beat Generation

American writers had a strong impact here, too. J. D. Salinger's *Catcher in the Rye* was the archetypal novel of adolescent defiance, angst and bloody-minded independence, but it was the group dismissively known as the 'beatniks' who perhaps made the greatest impression on pre-Sixties British youngsters of a literary and political bent.

Money talks

Barely a third of UK homes had television when the first commercial channel was introduced on 22 September 1955. (The very first ad was for Gibbs S.R. toothpaste.) The BBC responded by having a major character in its radio serial *The Archers* die in a fire that same evening, pulling a record audience of 20 million.

Within a few years ITV would have as large an audience as the BBC, but in those innocent times some parents refused to let their children tune in to it, as they felt that advertising was a distasteful business.

Angry young men

John Osborne's play *Look Back in Anger* was first performed at the Royal Court Theatre in London in 1956. Its working-class antihero, Jimmy Porter, spends much of the play railing against middle-class mediocrity.

Critics used to the more polite works of Noel Coward and Terence Rattigan were generally dismissive of it, referring to Osborne and a group of other young English writers as 'angry young men'.

The label fitted few of them – but this upsetting of the Establishment applecart can be seen as a forerunner of the furore that was to erupt over Sixties satire (see Chapter 2).

A number of the Beat poets – among them Allen Ginsberg (author of 'Howl', 1955) and Gregory Corso – would later take part in a memorable event in Sixties London. Ginsberg listed what he thought the movement was about:

- **Spiritual and sexual liberation.**
- **Liberation of the word from censorship.**
- **Decriminalisation of marijuana and other drugs.**
- **The evolution of rhythm and blues into rock and roll as a high art form.**
- **The spread of ecological consciousness.**
- **Opposition to the military–industrial machine civilisation.**
- **Respect for land and indigenous peoples and creatures.**

Notable among the Beat novelists were William S. Burroughs, whose scabrous *Naked Lunch* was published in 1959, and Jack Kerouac, whose *On the Road* (1957) inspired a generation of would-be footloose idealists with its account of road trips taken across the States by Sal Paradise and his charismatic, pot-smoking buddy Dean Moriarty.

'I read *On the Road* in maybe 1959. It changed my life like it changed everyone else's.'

Bob Dylan

The British had no writer like Kerouac, but there was some faint equivalence between the Beats' individualistic political stance and the anti-Establishment attitudes of the working-class heroes who appeared in novels by such as Alan Sillitoe, John Braine, David Storey and Stan Barstow. Something was stirring down below, and the times would soon be a-changin'.

Teddy Boys

In 1956 Frankie Lymon and the Teenagers had a hit with their song 'I'm not a juvenile delinquent.' It was a vacuous number but a timely one, because there were growing fears on both sides of the Atlantic that the disrespectful young were getting out of hand.

British tastes tended to follow the American lead at some distance, but the so-called Teddy Boys represented the first flowering of a distinctive youth culture. They dressed in a style vaguely derived from dandies during the 1901–1910 reign of Edward VII. The worst of them – mercifully a minority – brandished coshes, knuckle-dusters and flick-knives and earned sensational media coverage for staging gang fights. It was the 'Teds' who broke up cinemas at showings of *The Blackboard Jungle*, and the sight of a group of them shouldering their way towards him would encourage any young lad in their path to step out of the way pretty smartly.

Their uniform consisted of long drape jackets with velvet collars, 'Slim Jim' or bootlace ties, fancy waistcoats, drainpipe trousers and crepe-soled suede shoes known as 'brothel creepers'. They wore their hair long and greasy, often with a quiff at the front and the sides swept back (with a heavy steel comb) to form a 'duck's arse', or DA, at the rear.

They often bought this expensive gear on the 'never-never' – that is, paid for it by instalments – but it was a sign of increasing affluence among the young that they could afford it at all.

fidel leads the way

Fidel Castro's overthrow of the Cuban dictator General Batista in January 1959 was a Fifties event which, with hindsight, feels like a Sixties one, even to the lack of consensus as to whether it was a blessing or a curse. It's no wonder that Castro's second-in-command, Che Guevara, became a Sixties icon.

The sight of Castro's small band of victorious guerrillas riding atop their tanks into Havana after defeating a much larger government army in the mountains vibrated a romantic nerve for left-leaning idealists – of which there were a great many at the time.

Some fifties icons

Music: Frank Sinatra, Ella Fitzgerald, Duke Ellington, Elvis Presley

Film: James Dean, Marlon Brando, Grace Kelly, Marilyn Monroe, Audrey Hepburn, Brigitte Bardot

Fashion: Christian Dior, Pierre Balmain

Literature: Arthur Miller, Tennessee Williams, Jack Kerouac, Norman Mailer, Iris Murdoch, John Osborne

Sport: Stanley Matthews, Len Hutton, Rocky Marciano, Sugar Ray Robinson

Into a new age

Such was the background to the Swinging Sixties, a decade in which newly prosperous teenagers would emerge from their chrysalises like gaudy butterflies; in which taboos of race and gender would be tested to breaking point; in which artistic life would flourish in myriad unpredictable ways; in which satirists would find their voices and political leaders bow to demands for radical change.

While this book concentrates on events in Britain, it also acknowledges the remarkable worldwide nature of these phenomena. Can they be convincingly 'explained'? Sociologists have done their best, but for those of us who were there at the time it really did feel as if, to echo the Thunderclap Newman number, there was 'something in the air'.

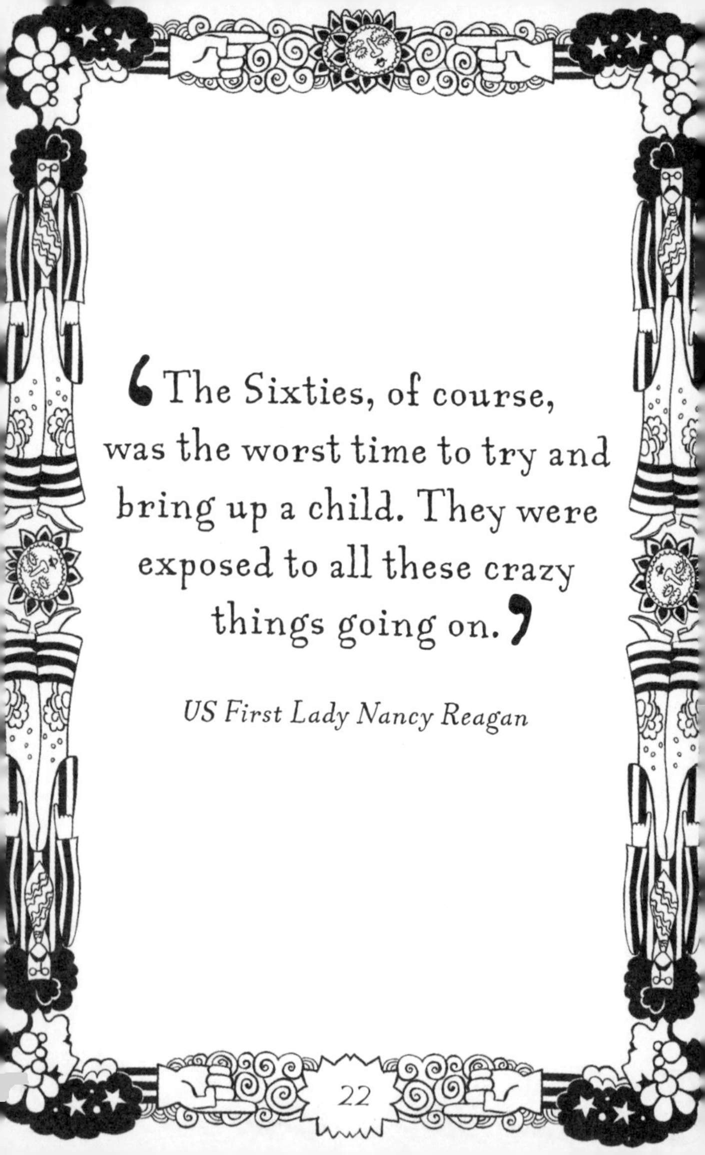

"The Sixties, of course, was the worst time to try and bring up a child. They were exposed to all these crazy things going on."

US First Lady Nancy Reagan

Chapter One

When Sexual Intercourse Began

It happened, Philip Larkin's poem claims with tongue-in-cheek precision, 'Between the end of the *Chatterley* ban [November 1960] / And the Beatles' first LP [March 1963]'.

Well, if the act itself had a rather longer history than that, it's certainly reasonable to argue that the obscenity trial of Penguin Books for publishing D. H. Lawrence's plain-speaking novel *Lady Chatterley's Lover* marked a significant step forwards (or backwards, depending upon your point of view) in the freedom to portray sexual matters frankly in a book of literary merit.

As a fitting curtain-raiser for the Sixties, the trial proved to be a wonderfully comic clash between the voices of old authority and the younger, 'permissive' generation eager to topple it. It followed the Obscene Publications Act of the previous year, piloted through Parliament by the young backbench MP (and later Labour home secretary) Roy Jenkins in an attempt to draw a line between illegal pornography and serious art and literature.

Twelve good men and true

Even as recently as the 1960s, juries weren't representative of the population as a whole: you could serve on one only if you were a property owner or tenant, and this disqualified a large swathe of women and young people.

Perhaps this was why Mervyn Griffith-Jones thought it sensible to talk to the jury about wives and servants – although after the Second World War very few people could imagine employing anyone to help in the home.

Under the Criminal Justice Act of 1972 qualifications for jury service were widened, becoming based on the right to vote.

Not in front of the servants

The prosecution's task was to prove that Lawrence's book, its explicit sex scenes accompanied by four-letter-word dialogue, was a filthy piece of work. Mervyn Griffith-Jones, the senior Treasury counsel representing the Crown, got off to a widely ridiculed start by suggesting questions which members of the jury should ask themselves.

'Would you', he asked, 'approve of your young sons, young daughters – because girls can read as well as boys – reading this book? . . . Is it a book that you would even wish your wife or your servants to read?'

Griffith-Jones had been one of the British prosecutors at the Nuremberg Trials, but he was horribly ill suited to this case. The Eton-educated barrister's son clearly found it hard to envisage a world without servants or submissive women – and he now had to overcome the stream of 35 eminent writers, critics and even bishops who stepped forward to praise the novel's qualities.

Few of them can have considered the book to be one of Lawrence's best, but there was a principle at stake, and distinguished writers E. M. Forster and Rebecca West, sociologist Richard Hoggart and future Poet Laureate Cecil Day-Lewis were among those who trooped into the witness box to defend its literary quality and its moral purpose.

The prize exhibit has to be the Bishop of Woolwich's written deposition to the court that 'Lawrence did not share the Christian valuation of sex, but he was always straining to portray it as something sacred, in a real sense as an act of Holy Communion.'

Although Penguin's founder, Allen Lane, had designed his paperbacks to be 'the same price as a packet of cigarettes', the response to the not-guilty verdict caught him by surprise. The initial run sold out overnight, and the novel clocked up sales of three million within just three months.

Not so lucky

Although the *Chatterley* trial had struck a blow for serious works of art, the law continued to deal severely with publications which lacked that protection. Indeed, another novel with a history of legal suppression (John Cleland's bawdy *Fanny Hill* of 1749) landed a London bookseller in the dock in 1964 – the publisher paid his costs. The defence argued that the book was a joyful celebration of normal, non-perverted sex, but the prosecution concentrated on a flagellation scene, and that was enough to swing the case. This victory, however, was illusory. The temper of the times had changed, and in 1970 an unexpurgated version would appear with no recriminations whatsoever.

Life was made especially difficult for the rash of little magazines which, in the boisterous spirit of the times, set out to expose, shock and antagonise authority. The stern blue eyes of Detective Inspector Frederick Luff, head of Scotland Yard's Obscene Publications Squad and notorious for his 'celebrity raids', were fixed upon every issue.

Liberal laws of the Sixties

- **Betting and Gaming Act 1960**
  It paved the way for betting shops and for slot machines in pubs. It also legalised gambling for small sums for games of skill. As the *Daily Telegraph* reported at the time, 'Weekly bridge clubs, meeting in the local hotel, will no longer have to settle up in the bus shelter.'

- **Race Relations Act 1965**
  This was the first legislation in the UK to address the 'colour bar', making it illegal to discriminate on the grounds 'of colour, race or ethnic or national origins' in public places. It prompted the creation of the Race Relations Board the following year. The legislation was refined in a new act three years later, which made it illegal to refuse housing, employment or public services to people because of their ethnic background.

- **Murder (Death Penalty Abolition) Act 1965**
  This was introduced to Parliament as a private member's bill, with a so-called sunset clause stating that it would be repealed in five years unless renewed by Parliament. The Act became permanent in 1969.

- **Abortion Act 1967**
  The new law legalised abortions by registered practitioners in England, Scotland and Wales (but not Northern Ireland), and regulated their provision through the National Health

Service. No longer would women have to risk death at the hands of untrained back-street abortionists. Introduced by David Steel as a private member's bill, the new act made abortion legal up to 28 weeks' gestation. The law was amended in 1990, reducing the time to 24 weeks except when the woman's life was in danger, she was under grave risk of physical or mental injury, or there was evidence of extreme foetal abnormality.

- **Sexual Offences Act 1967**
  This law decriminalised homosexual acts in private between two men, both of whom had reached the age of 21. It applied only to England and Wales, and didn't cover the Merchant Navy or the armed forces.

- **Theatres Act 1968**
  Critic Kenneth Tynan and playwright John Osborne were key figures in the framing of this legislation, which removed censorship by the Lord Chamberlain's office – a state of affairs that had existed since 1737.

- **Divorce Reform Act 1969**
  The Act restated the three existing grounds for divorce defined as 'faults' (adultery, cruelty and desertion) and added two 'no-fault separation grounds' based on a couple having lived apart for a specified number of years.

Private Eye

That great survivor amongst the satirical magazines, *Private Eye,* first saw the light of day in October 1961. It developed from a school magazine, and those who dismissed it evidently felt that it had never escaped that pedigree. Equally, one imagines, its earliest luminaries, Christopher Booker, Willie Rushton and Richard Ingrams, would have been happy to acknowledge its mixture of waywardness and sheer silliness, mixed as it was with a steadily increasing satirical bite.

The *Eye* has been taken to court on countless occasions and has narrowly avoided bankruptcy. It was, perhaps, a badge of honour that the high street newsagents W. H. Smith refused to stock the magazine throughout the Sixties and beyond. (The firm was inevitably tagged 'W. H. Smut' by the magazine, because of the top-shelf publications it did sell.) A badge of *dis*honour, in retrospect, was its decidedly unprogressive insistence on referring to the gay movement as 'poove power'.

The *Eye*'s strength, then as now, was that it attracted first-class journalists on mainstream papers who were eager to write stories which, true as they might be, couldn't get past the blue pencils of their own sub-editors.

Dirty work

It didn't become clear until years later that the Obscene Publications Squad was itself mired in corruption throughout the time that it was hounding publishers during the Sixties.

In 1976 the squad was completely reformed after a series of trials revealed that it had been running a massive bribery racket since its inception in 1960. As much as £1,000 a month had been handed over by traders in hardcore pornography in return for leniency by the police.

Justice Mars-Jones found that much of the pornography seized by the squad had been shamelessly 'sold back into the trade'.

IT

While *Private Eye* was awash with former public schoolboys, the *International Times* (changed to *IT* after *The Times* threatened a lawsuit) was resolutely underground.

It was launched in October 1966 at a Roundhouse event in London which featured 'steel bands, strips, trips, happenings, movies'. Daevid Allen, guitarist of the acid band Soft Machine, which played there alongside Pink Floyd, claimed that it was 'one of the two most revolutionary events in the history of English alternative music and thinking,' and marked 'the first recognition of a rapidly spreading socio-cultural revolution that had its parallel in the States'. (That's how they spoke then.)

Its content (sex, drugs, rock and roll) had a genuine international reach. Of course this content antagonised Det. Insp. Luff, and *IT* was often 'visited' – prompting a reprisal raid on New Scotland Yard by another underground magazine, *Black Dwarf,* which not only got inside, but revealed details of the Met's security arrangements.

Oz

Richard Neville founded this magazine in Australia in 1963. It took a strong line against police corruption, and the following year Neville and two of his colleagues were jailed for six months with hard labour for obscenity. The convictions were overturned on appeal, chiefly because the judge was found to have misdirected the jury.

In 1967 Neville launched *Oz* in London. The edition which saw him and his co-editors Jim Anderson and Felix Dennis charged with 'conspiracy to corrupt public morals' falls just outside our period. The 'Schoolkids' *Oz*' of May 1970 was designed by young volunteers, and the chief prosecutor said that it dealt with 'homosexuality, lesbianism, sadism, perverted sexual practices and drug taking'. Once again a prison sentence was handed down, and once again an appeal succeeded because of misdirection by the judge, but not before prison officers had shaved the three men's long hair – that classic Sixties symbol of freedom and non-conformity. This act of vengeance provoked a public outcry.

Beyond the fringe

The four young men who wrote and performed the stage revue *Beyond the Fringe* (first seen in 1960) were the forerunners of later satirists without having a sharp political edge themselves.

Alan Bennett, Peter Cook, Jonathan Miller and Dudley Moore were former Oxbridge students with an offbeat sense of humour and a delight in pricking the pomposity of the older generation.

They could certainly offend. Some took their piece 'The Aftermyth of War' as an attack on brave soldiers, though it was intended as a send-up of empty patriotic attitudes.

Prime Minister Harold Macmillan, who had the temerity to attend one of their performances, was offended by Cook's parody of his faux upper-class mannerisms. Cook, knowing that he was in the audience, simply twisted the knife a little further.

Their iconoclasm inspired the work of two later groups of entertainers: the wounding satire of *That Was The Week That Was* (1962–1963) and the zaniness of *Monty Python's Flying Circus* (1969–1974).

Too near the knuckle

One of the features in the offending issue of *Oz* was a highly sexualised treatment of the children's cartoon character Rupert Bear. Sex had always been a hang-up with the British, and during the Sixties those who were particularly uneasy about it found it just about everywhere they looked.

Even the Tory government seemed to be colluding with the permissive society, for goodness' sake! Enoch Powell would later be known for his illiberal views on immigration, but in December 1961, as Minister of Health, it was he who sanctioned the prescription of contraceptive pills at a subsidised price on the National Health Service. True, this was for married women only, but everyone knew what would happen next. Those pills were out of the bottle.

'The freedom that women were supposed to have found in the Sixties largely boiled down to easy contraception and abortion; things to make life easier for men, in fact.'

Feminist writer Julie Burchill

Enter Mary Whitehouse

The forces of reaction to this increasingly orthodox laxity were galvanised by a doughty woman who refused to be cowed by the ridicule she inevitably attracted. Mary Whitehouse was no prude, but an earnest Christian of conservative bent who taught art and sex education and was shocked by the standards of her young charges. She aimed her weapons at the BBC in particular, founding the Clean Up TV pressure group in 1964 and a year later replacing it with the more aggressive National Viewers' and Listeners' Association. She accused the Corporation's director general, Sir Hugh Greene, of being 'more than anyone else' responsible for the country's moral decline, his organisation spreading 'the propaganda of disbelief, doubt and dirt . . . promiscuity, infidelity and drinking'.

Greene, who spoke darkly of censorship and refused to bow to her demands, privately commissioned a portrait of her from the expressionist artist James Lawrence Isherwood; it shows her with five breasts.

Mrs Whitehouse continued to campaign for many years. During the Sixties she seemed to be fighting a losing battle, but we can now see that she landed a number of effective blows along the way.

The ineffable Tynan

The brilliant and flamboyant critic Kenneth Tynan took exhibitionism to the extreme during a live TV debate in November 1965. Discussing sexual explicitness on stage, he said he doubted that many people would find the F-word totally out of bounds – using the word itself for the very first time on television.

The uproar was unsurprising, although Mary Whitehouse excelled herself by writing to the Queen about it. She suggested to Her Majesty that he should have 'his bottom spanked', presumably unaware that flagellation happened to be one of Tynan's vices.

Drugs busts

If sex was top of the shock list for soap-box moralists, drugs ran it a pretty close second. Cannabis had been the Beat Poets' choice of mood changer and perception enhancer, and in Sixties Britain its use had become commonplace in the so-called counterculture.

Here are a few of its pet names:

- **Marijuana**
- **Mary Jane**
- **Pot**
- **Hash**
- **Weed**
- **Dope**

'If you remember the Sixties,
you weren't there.'

Variously attributed

Broken butterflies

Needless to say, the police often came visiting, the most notorious episode being a raid on the Sussex home of the Rolling Stones guitarist Keith Richards one night in 1967. Hauled before the courts, Richards was sentenced to a year in jail for allowing cannabis to be smoked in his house, while lead singer Mick Jagger was sent down for three months for possessing four amphetamine tablets, or 'pep pills'.

For good measure, detectives raided the home of another band member, Brian Jones, while the trial was under way, and he was imprisoned for drugs possession too.

The severity of these sentences appalled even that organ of respectability *The Times*. Its editor, William Rees-Mogg, slightly misquoting the 18th-century poet Alexander Pope, asked: 'Who breaks a butterfly on a wheel?' and suggested that the musicians had been treated much more severely than had they been ordinary members of the public.

All three Stones would have their prison sentences quashed, but not before 64 public figures had put their signatures to an advertisement in *The Times* which stated that 'The law against marijuana is immoral in principle and unworkable in practice.'

Paul McCartney paid for the ad, but although the Beatles and their manager Brian Epstein signed up to it, the list was broadly based and predominantly non-hippie, including such substantial names as the writer Graham Greene, the broadcaster David Dimbleby, the psychiatrists David Stafford-Clark and Anthony Storr, the publisher Tom Maschler and the DNA scientist Dr Francis Crick.

'Lucy in the Sky with Diamonds'

Though the battle to legalise pot was lost, the campaign probably contributed to a more tolerant attitude towards its use in the years ahead. It's doubtful, though, that many of its respectable champions would have similarly rallied round that other 'signature' drug of the Sixties, LSD.

In a 2004 interview, Paul McCartney admitted that a number of the Beatles' songs made 'subtle hints' about drugs. 'A song like "Got to Get You Into My Life", that's directly about pot,' he said, 'although everyone missed it at the time. "Day Tripper", that's one about acid. "Lucy in the Sky", that's pretty obvious.'

'Turn on, tune in, drop out'

This was the mantra of Dr Timothy Leary, a lecturer in psychology at Harvard University who began experimenting with LSD in 1960 after previously enjoying the experience of eating hallucinogenic mushrooms during a trip to Mexico.

The drug wasn't yet illegal, but, to the consternation of the university, Leary involved students in his researches, and in an interview with *Playboy* magazine he claimed that it was a potent aphrodisiac. He lost his job. In 1964, with another fired professor, Richard Alpert, he published *The Psychedelic Experience: A Manual Based on the Tibetan Book of the Dead.*

From this time Leary's interest in LSD became more recreational than scientific. A judge gave him 30 years in jail for possessing half a cannabis reefer (the Supreme Court unsurprisingly overturned the sentence), while President Nixon described him as 'the most dangerous man in America'.

'We saw ourselves', Leary said later, 'as anthropologists from the twenty-first century inhabiting a time module set somewhere in the Dark Ages of the 1960s. On this space colony we were attempting to create a new paganism and a new dedication to life as art.'

Marijuana increased the heart rate, lowered the blood pressure and (being less strong than the stuff sold on the streets today) reduced many of its users to slumbrous philosophising. LSD was a different animal altogether, promising its takers a colourful roller-coaster of images and emotions.

British psychiatrist Humphry Fortescue Osmond (1917–2004) coined the word *psychedelic* to cover LSD and other hallucinogens he experimented with. He was a friend of *Brave New World* author Aldous Huxley (1894–1963), whose *Doors of Perception* chronicled his own experience of taking mescalin. Huxley sent Osmond a celebratory couplet:

> To make this mundane world sublime,
> Take half a gram of phanerothyme.

Osmond responded in similar vein:

> To fathom Hell or soar angelic
> Just take a pinch of psychedelic.

Huxley felt these powerful drugs should be entrusted to intellectuals only, but now psychedelic colours were everywhere – even in the vibrant patterns followed by dogged knitters of comfy home-made sweaters.

Sixties mystics

Sublimity, Hell and angels bring us to another Sixties phenomenon: the period's earnest quest for some kind of spiritual fulfilment beyond the rigid confines of what many saw as old-style, outworn Western religion. (John Lennon told a reporter in 1966 that the Beatles were now more popular than Jesus – a remark that failed to cause a stir in the UK but led to public burnings of the group's records in the United States and elsewhere.)

Aldous Huxley thought that acid's gifts ranged from pure aesthetic pleasure to 'sacramental vision', and in South California (just the place for this kind of thing) he sat at the feet of Swami Prabhavananda of the Vedanta Society.

The Beatles' yearnings were sublimated by another Indian mystic, Maharishi Mahesh Yogi, who developed the technique known as transcendental meditation and (to some mirth outside his own circle) would later advocate that his disciples should practise levitation in the pursuit of world peace.

Some secular gurus

- **Marshall McLuhan**
His phrase 'The medium is the message' was one of the buzzwords of the Sixties – and gave rise to the punning title of his best-selling 1967 book, *The Medium Is the Massage*. McLuhan, a Canadian critic and communication theorist, taught that the technology we use (the medium) becomes part of our thinking processes. He coined the expression 'the global village' and predicted the World Wide Web decades before it was invented.

- **R. D. Laing**
The Scottish psychiatrist specialised in mental illnesses, and (though he disliked the label) was regarded as a major figure in the anti-psychiatry movement. He rejected the notion that psychosis was essentially a biological phenomenon, and sought to place a patient's difficulties within his or her social, intellectual and cultural background. Schizophrenia, he argued, was a theory rather than a fact. Madness was often an expression of social distress, and should be valued as a cathartic and transformative experience.

- **Herbert Marcuse**
A German Jewish philosopher and political theorist who became a US citizen in 1940, Marcuse was the darling of the Sixties student movement because of his willingness to speak at their protests. He was a lifelong Marxist who (although he hated the term)

became known as 'the father of the New Left'. His 1969 *Essay on Liberation* inspired fellow radicals, although *Counterrevolution and Revolt*, which followed it, warned that Sixties ideals were under threat from the right.

- **Jacques Lacan**
The French psychoanalyst and psychiatrist influenced a raft of Sixties intellectuals, in particular the post-structuralist philosophers who were rather more honoured than read – outside the universities at least. He had an impact on critical, literary, film and feminist theory, as well as clinical psychoanalysis. Lacan was an unashamed Freudian, his work featuring the unconscious, the ego and the castration complex. Regarded as belonging to the far left, he expressed his sympathy with Sixties student protests in France.

Psychedelic Review

This magazine, founded in 1963, was a scholarly rather than an underground publication, but some of its early essay titles reflect the spirit of the times:

- **Can this drug enlarge man's mind?**
- **Herman Hesse: poet of the interior journey**
- **The god in the flowerpot**
- **Shouted from the housetops: A peyote awakening**
- **Hallucinations as the world of spirits.**

The Maharishi was opposed to drugs, but many a seeker after truth and self-knowledge swore by them. In the United States (indeed, in California again), *One Flew Over the Cuckoo's Nest* author Ken Kesey staged parties which he called 'acid tests', involving wild music, fluorescent paint, strobe lighting and other psychedelic effects heightened by the ingestion of LSD. Not everyone survived unscathed.

In 1964 Kesey and his Merry Pranksters painted a school bus in DayGlo colours and travelled east to New York, dispensing LSD along the way. (It wouldn't be banned in America until October 1966.) At the wheel was Neal Cassady, the model for Jack Kerouac's Dean Moriarty in *On the Road* and described by novelist Robert Stone as 'the world's greatest driver, who could roll a joint while backing a 1937 Packard onto the lip of the Grand Canyon'.

The trek's legendary status was bolstered by the publication of journalist Tom Wolfe's *The Electric Kool-Aid Acid Test* four years later.

The hippie trail

In the 18th century every young aristocrat was expected to take the Grand Tour, savouring cultured Europe and bringing back trophies to grace his ancient family pile. During the Sixties it was the turn of young dropouts, both male and female, who (a cheap *BIT Guide* for travellers in their rucksacks) hitch-hiked or jumped on cheap buses to visit India, Pakistan, Nepal and other parts of southern Asia. They brought back memories.

Most of the young adventurers passed through Istanbul, with some then taking a northern route to India via Tehran, Kabul and Lahore, while Pakistan-bound travellers crossed Syria, Jordan, Iraq and Iran. Kathmandu was a favourite destination; one of its thoroughfares is still popularly known as Freak Street in doubtful tribute to the many thousands of footloose Westerners who once passed along it.

Books about the experience include *Magic Bus* by Rory Maclean, *Wrong Way Home* by Peter Moore, and Paul Theroux's *The Great Railway Bazaar*, which tells of his four-month trip across Asia by train, the first part of it following the hippie trail.

The Summer of Love

If you had to boil the general yearning down to a single word you couldn't do better than fix on 'love' – a flimsy concept at the best of times, but one that seemed to suffice for the hundred thousand people who flocked to the Haight-Ashbury district of San Francisco during the 'Summer of Love' in 1967, and for the millions in the rest of America and across the world who sang that universal hymn to 'flower power' along with Scott McKenzie:

> If you're going to San Francisco,
> Be sure to wear some flowers in your hair.
> If you're going to San Francisco,
> You're gonna meet some gentle people there.

Down the coast in Monterey that summer massive crowds flocked to the world's first heavily promoted rock festival, featuring Jimi Hendrix, Janis Joplin, Otis Redding and groups such as The Grateful Dead, The Doors, Jefferson Airplane and The Byrds.

Honest to God

Even the Church of England was forced to take a look at its own beliefs after a book by the Bishop of Woolwich, John Robinson – defender of the 'holy communion' sex scenes in *Lady's Chatterley's Lover* – became an overnight sensation.

Honest to God was written in 1963 and clocked up sales of 300,000 copies in three months. Robinson denied abandoning his Christianity (as his critics claimed), but argued for a new theology to suit the modern age. Rather than being 'out there', he wrote, God should – in the words of existentialist theologian Paul Tillich – be regarded as 'the ground of our being'.

His idea that God's revelation to humanity could be experienced within the wider culture rather than in the narrow confines of the Church was hardly likely to endear him to the authorities, and the Archbishop of Canterbury wrote a pamphlet denouncing the book. In later years both men took the view that it had been a storm in a teacup, but at least the Anglican church had had its Sixties moment.

Mods and Rockers

Not all the young were conscious rebels. Many of them, however much they picked up the general vibes, simply wanted to have a good time – and so the Mod movement was born in the UK.

The Mods were young people who suddenly had enough money to go out and enjoy themselves in a way their parents could never have imagined. We'll catch up with their fashions later: suffice it to say here that they were sharply suited and liked to scoot around on low-powered Lambretta and Vespa two-wheelers dangling mirrors and mascots.

And drugs? They had a particular fancy for 'purple hearts', an amphetamine–barbiturate combination. These were tossed back not to send the mind on a trip to some technicolour nirvana, but to keep the body going through long hours on the dance floor. These Mods were above all eager party-goers.

Thanks to a series of clashes during holiday weekends in the mid-Sixties they are now for ever remembered as part of a riotous double act with the Rockers, leather-jacketed, greasy-haired roughs on noisy motorbikes who were everything the fastidious Mods were not.

Their choice of music was different, too. The Rockers – Teddy Boys on wheels – liked Elvis Presley, Gene Vincent and Eddie Cochran. The Mods were into R&B, soul, Jamaican ska and British bands such as The Who, The Kinks and The Small Faces.

A *Clockwork Orange*

Anthony Burgess described his 1962 novel as 'a sort of allegory of Christian free will'. Set in a near-future England, it tells the story of a band of teenage thugs who indulge in nightly orgies of violence.

The final, redemptive chapter was cut from the American edition of the book, and the subsequent film by Stanley Kubrick followed this version and seemed to glorify its characters' worst excesses.

Burgess said he regretted ever writing the book: 'In a film little can be implied,' he said. 'Everything has to be shown.'

The trouble kicked off at Clacton-on-Sea, Essex, on the 1964 Easter bank holiday weekend. The weather was wet and miserable, the place had practically closed down and the thousand visiting Mods had nothing to do. They took their boredom out on the pier (stallholders swiftly shut up shop), damaged beach huts along the front and threw deck chairs through shop windows. A small gaggle of Rockers was chased along the streets.

The 60 policemen on duty that day made 97 arrests (two dozen youngsters were charged with minor offences), but they brought in reinforcements the following day, suspecting that there was worse to come. Nothing much happened, in fact, but the media had already seized on the potential drama, and the *Daily Mirror* ran a headline that Monday morning which nodded towards a Fifties biker film starring the surly Marlon Brando:

'WILD ONES' INVADE SEASIDE

Sawdust Caesars

The subsequent chain of events now seems inevitable. Over the following months Mods and Rockers flocked to south-coast resorts such as Margate, Brighton and Bournemouth, engaged in fisticuffs (and sometimes worse) and were widely condemned in the media and in Parliament as the nation seemed overcome by a surfeit of what the sociologist Stanley Cohen called 'moral panic'.

A magistrate in Margate had his moment of fame after one fracas, being widely quoted for describing the town's unwanted visitors as 'these long-haired, mentally unstable, petty little hoodlums, these sawdust Caesars who can only find courage like rats, in hunting in packs'.

The home secretary, Henry Brooke, not only rushed a Malicious Damages Bill through Parliament, but put 69 officers from Scotland Yard's flying squad on red alert at RAF Northolt, ready to cope with any emergency. Sure enough there was trouble at Hastings the very next Sunday afternoon, and the eager cops were flown in to deal with what the press couldn't resist calling 'the Battle of Hastings'.

As always on such occasions the immediate sentences were out of proportion to the offences themselves, including prison terms and heavy fines, but they sent out a strong signal. Perhaps because of this, or perhaps because the novelty had worn off, the Mods and Rockers soon abandoned their seaside

Quadrophenia

The most notorious Mods and Rockers confrontation was at Brighton during the 1964 May bank holiday, when two people were stabbed during a series of running fights along the seafront.

The Who's rock opera *Quadrophenia* tells the story of a London Mod, Jimmy Cooper, who has taken part in the Brighton fracas but who is dispirited to discover when he returns to the town a little later that the Mod phenomenon is already on the wane.

Quadrophenia was later turned into a film, loosely based on the original.

lawlessness to seek their pleasures elsewhere. At the height of the trouble Frank Taylor MP had asked the government 'to give urgent and serious consideration to the need for young hooligans to be given such financial and physical punishment as will provide an effective deterrent,' while the Earl of Arran tabled a motion in the House of Lords calling for the raising of the minimum driving licence age from 16 to 19 in order to keep all those young two-wheelers off the roads.

But had the older generation not recently blotted its own copybook? Had an MP and a member of the House of Lords not been involved in the biggest sex-and-politics scandal of the decade? The young had hardly been set a good example…

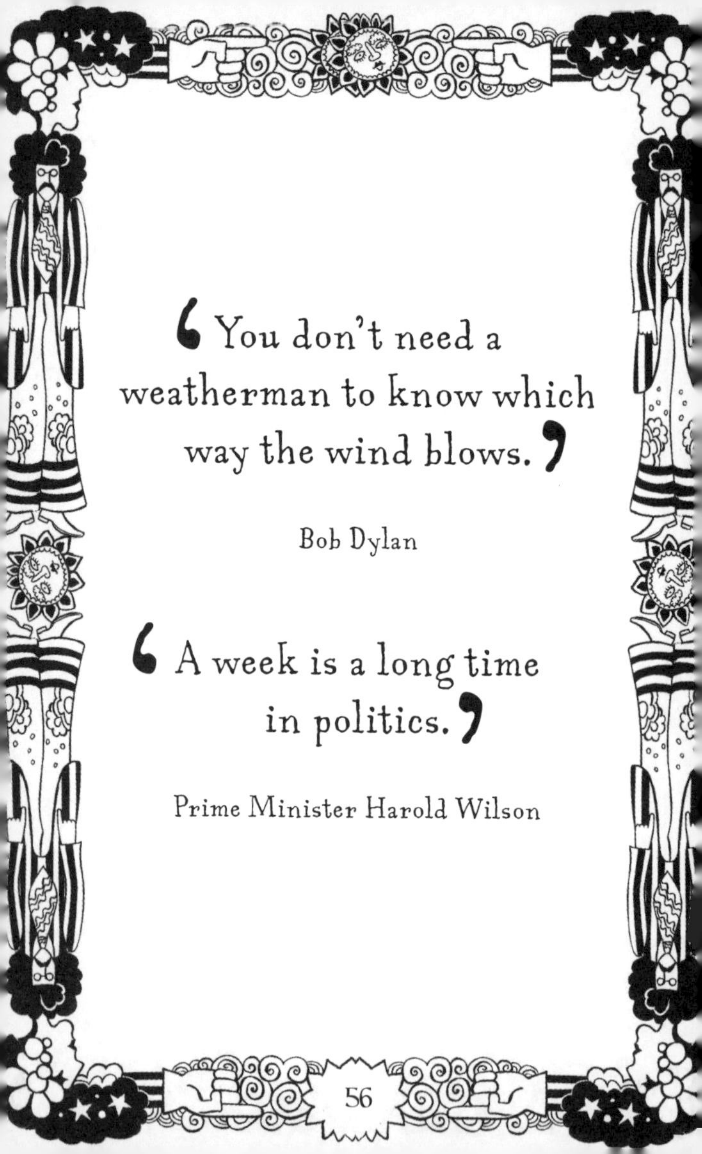

‘You don’t need a weatherman to know which way the wind blows.’

Bob Dylan

‘A week is a long time in politics.’

Prime Minister Harold Wilson

CHAPTER TWO

THAT WAS THE DECADE THAT WAS

In the sweltering heat of a July day in 1961, John Profumo, secretary of state for war, watched a leggy girl rise naked from the swimming pool at Viscount Astor's opulent Buckinghamshire estate, Cliveden – and so began the lurid sexual scandal which finished his political career, indirectly put her in gaol, and provoked another of its miscellaneous cast of characters to commit suicide.

The naked apparition was Christine Keeler, an easy-living 19-year-old showgirl. Within days she and Profumo had become lovers, a liaison which sent the undercover agents of MI5 into overdrive. This was about to become a political scandal, too.

> 'There is a ghastly unreality about it all... To own it, to live here, would be like living on the stage of the Scala theatre in Milan.'
>
> *Cliveden described by diplomat Harold Nicolson*

The problem was that Keeler had also been sharing her favours with Yevgeny Ivanov, a senior naval attaché (or intelligence officer) at the Soviet Embassy. At the height of Cold War paranoia, who knew what dangerous pillow talk might be passed to the Russians?

MI5 also had its beady eyes on Stephen Ward, a Harley Street osteopath and portrait painter with glittering connections. In India he had treated Gandhi for headaches and a stiff neck, while his many illustrious English clients included Sir Winston Churchill, no less. Viscount Astor, another of them, allowed Ward the use of a cottage in his dramatically landscaped grounds at Cliveden; Keeler had been staying with him there when

Profumo saw her by the pool. Ivanov was one of Ward's friends.

The Ward/Cliveden set enjoyed wild sex parties, many of them arranged by the notorious Mariella Novotny (because so many senior politicians attended them, she referred to herself as the government's chief whip), but it was the espionage angle which finally brought the Profumo story into the open in 1963. The Labour MP George Wigg drew Parliament's attention to media rumours, adding that 'The Press has got as near as it can – it has shown itself willing to wound but afraid to strike.'

In those still timorous times Fleet Street had indeed fretted about how much it could reveal. Nudges and winks were permitted, but they would surely have meant little to the man and woman in the street.

On the very day that Wigg raised the issue in the House of Commons, *Private Eye* had made oblique references to 'a West Indian immigrant of no fixed abode'; to the proffered, and refused, resignation of 'Mr James

Montesi, a well-known Cabinet Minister'; and to parties arranged by a 'Dr Spook' which involved 'Mr Vladimir Bolokhov, the well-known Soviet spy attached to the Russian Embassy, and a well-known Cabinet Minister'.

Wigg was more specific. The rumour, he said, 'relates to Miss Christine Keeler and Miss Davies and a shooting by a West Indian', and he called for a select committee to be set up so that 'the honour of the minister concerned might be freed from innuendoes'.

It's time to catch up with a few more of the *dramatis personae*:

- **Mandy Rice-Davies.** A friend of Keeler's, a model and part of the same fun-loving set.
- **Aloysius 'Lucky' Gordon.** A Jamaican jazz pianist and singer, and one of Keeler's former lovers. She alleged that in the aftermath of their affair he attacked her and held her hostage for two days.
- **Johnny Edgecombe.** An Antiguan hustler, and another of Keeler's lovers. He attacked Gordon with a knife at the Flamingo Club in Wardour Street, London, in October 1962,

and the following December fired shots outside Stephen Ward's flat where Keeler and Rice-Davies were staying. This incident brought in the police and had the effect of opening the whole can of worms.

- **Slum landlord Peter Rachman and fraudulent businessman Emil Savundra.** Neither was connected with the Profumo case, but both were named by Rice-Davies as former lovers when she gave evidence in court.

Profumo, whose offer to resign had indeed been rejected by prime minister Harold Macmillan, came to the Commons and made a statement saying that there had been 'no impropriety whatsoever' in his relationship with Christine Keeler, and that he would take legal action if the newspapers suggested otherwise. He then went off to the races in the company of his wife (the actress Valerie Hobson) and that keen habituée of the track, the Queen Mother.

The reprieve was brief. Ward gave the home secretary evidence that Profumo and Keeler had been lovers, and the disgraced MP resigned – not, of course, for the affair itself, but because he had lied to Parliament.

A rash of trials

Three trials followed. In the first, Lucky Gordon was jailed for attacking Christine Keeler, while in the third, six months later, Keeler was sent down for nine months for perjury after admitting that she had lied about the assault all along. (Gordon was freed as a result.)

Between these two cases the public had to watch the unedifying spectacle of Stephen Ward's prosecution for living off immoral earnings – specifically for procuring girls under the age of 21 to have sexual intercourse, for procuring abortions, and for keeping a brothel. This felt like an act of revenge by the wounded Establishment, an impression strengthened by the choice of Mervyn Griffith-Jones of *Lady Chatterley* trial fame as prosecutor.

Ward, acquitted of procuring but found guilty of pimping for Keeler and Rice-Davies, never heard the verdict. He had taken an overdose of sleeping tablets and died in hospital a few days later. At his funeral there was a wreath of a hundred white carnations sent by leading figures in the arts world: critic Kenneth Tynan, novelist and critic Penelope Gilliat, singer and actress Annie Ross, portrait painter Dominic Elwes, and the playwrights John Osborne, Arnold Wesker and Joe Orton. Their card read:

To Stephen Ward
Victim of Hypocrisy

'He would, wouldn't he?'

Mandy Rice-Davies (or Randy Mice-Davies, as satirists liked to call her) showed no squeamishness when talking about her sex life during the Stephen Ward trial, and happily provided a list of her many lovers.

One of her remarks, simple as it was, has survived as a catch-phrase to be used in any appropriate situation.

When it was pointed out that Lord Astor had denied any involvement with her, her swift reply was devastating: 'Well, he would, wouldn't he?' (*laughter in court*).

And what happened to the other members of the cast?

- **John Profumo,** his wife standing by him, retired to a life of charity work, and in 1975 was awarded the CBE for his involvement with the disadvantaged in the East End of London.

- **Christine Keeler** wrote and co-authored several books about her life and the Profumo affair. She later worked in telephone sales, for a dry-cleaning business and as a school dinner lady.

- **Mandy Rice-Davies** sang, acted and wrote books, including an autobiography, married an Israeli and set up a chain of 'Mandy' clubs in Israel. Her life, she once said, had followed 'one slow descent into respectability'.

TW3

'What the hell is going on in this country?' the *Daily Mirror* asked in the wake of Profumo's resignation, adding that 'All power corrupts and the Tories have been in power for nearly twelve years.' The *Times*, countering the view that the sexual shenanigans were an irrelevance, carried the headline IT IS A MORAL ISSUE, while the bishop of Southwark, Mervyn Stockwood, wrote that the events had left behind them 'an unpleasant smell – the smell of corruption in high places, of evil practices, and of a repudiation of the simple decencies and the basic values'.

In this climate, it's no wonder that BBC television's live satire show *That Was The Week That Was* – shortened to *TWTWTW* and even more economically to *TW3* – was welcomed as a veritable cleansing of the Augean stables. Launched in November 1962, it ran for only two seasons, but its irreverent attack on hypocrisy and cant, its fearless locking of horns with royalty, religions and corrupt businessmen, made it an unmissable Saturday-night event for millions.

The old order changeth

The shifts in a culture's tectonic plates are felt in trivial matters as much as in grand political developments...

- During the early Sixties it was commonplace for cinemas to play the national anthem at the end of each performance – although audiences were showing an increasing reluctance to stand up for it and some vacated their seats early to avoid it.

- The passing of a hearse was still an occasion for the public to stop in their tracks, remove their hats if they were wearing them, and lower their heads in respect – but the press of traffic soon made the crawling pace of funeral cars impractical.

- National Service narrowly survived into the new decade, with the last man 'called up' on the last day of 1960. Mind you, this only encouraged older folk to repeat the tedious mantra that a couple of years in the army wouldn't do today's youngsters any harm!

- It took the threat of a strike by the players for the Football League to abolish the maximum wage in 1961. During the previous year the average national wage had been £15 a week, with the players getting a top whack of £20. Johnny Haynes of Fulham and England now became the first £100-a-week player.

- In September 1962 the last Gentlemen v. Players cricket match was played, at Scarborough. 'Gentlemen', usually from middle-class backgrounds, were amateurs, and 'players' were professionals. From this time the concept of amateurism – 'a ludicrous system', said the plain-speaking Yorkshire bowler Fred Trueman – was abolished.
- On 3 May 1966 *The Times* at last began printing news on its front page (it had made an exception only to report Winston Churchill's funeral the previous year). The page had previously been given over to advertisements, a dullness which was now considered out of synch with… the times.

There had never been anything like *TW3*. If *Private Eye* had broken the ground for the programme with its wickedly deflating humour, *TW3* brandished sharper weaponry altogether, and it inevitably angered those it wounded – not only politicians but, for example, the Boy Scout Association, which objected to the questioning of Lord Baden-Powell's sexuality.

Mary Whitehouse, unsurprisingly, regarded it as 'the epitome of what was wrong with the BBC – anti-authority, anti-religious, anti-patriotism, pro-dirt, and poorly produced . . . and apparently impervious to discipline from within or disapproval from without'.

Poorly produced? The studio paraphernalia – mics, cameras, cables and so on – were all on view, and the performers would often read from scripts, giving *TW3* a brash, 'genuine' atmosphere. Again, this was new and exciting.

The programme was presented by the former Methodist lay preacher David Frost, who would eventually become something of an Establishment figure himself. Its list of script writers was impressive, including among others Peter Cook, journalist Keith Waterhouse, Kenneth Tynan, playwright Dennis Potter, John Cleese and even the future poet laureate John Betjeman. The cast included Willie Rushton, Frankie Howerd, Eleanor Bron, John Wells, the cartoonist Timothy Birdsall and the commentator Bernard Levin.

Each programme began with a topical number sung by Millicent Martin, while Lance Percival would improvise a calypso to topical suggestions from the audience. Timings weren't vital, because the show was open-ended. (When the BBC *did* try to fix a closing time by scheduling repeats of *The Third Man* after it, Frost read synopses of what was to follow by way of a spoiler; the Corporation caved in.)

The idea of a prime minister being lampooned on national television was almost shocking, but Harold Macmillan came in for regular mockery – and, it has to be said, manfully took it on the chin. The Profumo affair was a low point (Frost appeared, apparently naked, on a chair, sending up the celebrated pose adopted by Christine Keeler in a publicity photograph), but the programme was also merciless in highlighting his delusions of grandeur over the 'special relationship' with the Americans.

'Hello, Jack,' he begins a telephone call to John F. Kennedy at the White House. 'This is Harold... Harold Macmillan... Macmillan... M-A-C-M...'

No holds barred

Unthinking respect for authority was on its knees. Nothing illustrates this more vividly than *Private Eye*'s treatment of a parliamentary speech in which Macmillan derided Labour for dithering and recited (in his upper-class drawl) the old music-hall number 'She Didn't Say Yes, She Didn't Say No.' Willie Rushton impersonated the old buffer to a musical backing on a record which sold throughout the country in huge numbers.

TW3 was last broadcast in December 1963, ostensibly because there was to be an election the following year and the BBC wished to ensure impartiality. The cynics noted that it also happened to be a year in which Parliament was due to debate the renewal of the Corporation's charter. Sir Hugh Carleton Green, its director general, later commented: 'It was in my capacity as a subversive anarchist that I yielded to the enormous pressure from my fellow subversives and put *TW3* on the air; and it was as a pillar of the Establishment that I yielded to the Fascist hyena-like howls to take it off again.'

The Night of the Long Knives

Harold Macmillan responded dramatically to the government's lack of popularity in July 1962 by sacking a third of his cabinet, including the chancellor of the exchequer – a bloodletting which immediately became known as the Night of the Long Knives after the murderous Nazi purge of 1934.

Liberal leader Jeremy Thorpe turned instead to the Bible, devastatingly inverting a line from St John's Gospel: 'Greater love hath no man than this, that he should lay down his friends for his life.'

Three men in a boat

Three prime ministers with contrasting personalities piloted the good ship *Britannia* through the choppy waters of the Sixties.

Harold Macmillan (Conservative, in office 1957–1963) played the part of a witty, unflappable Edwardian gentleman. This role did not equip him well to cope with the Profumo scandal, which he was generally thought to have mishandled. In his early years as PM he was 'Supermac', after a cartoon by Vicky in the *Evening Standard* – an image not intended to flatter, but which suited him when the economy was buoyant and the country more at ease with itself. He faltered during the early Sixties, and took the opportunity of a minor health scare to step down and return to the family publishing business. His personal tragedy was the long-standing liaison of his wife Dorothy with a fellow Tory, Lord (Bob) Boothby.

Sir Alec Douglas-Home (Conservative, 1963–1964). The Peerage Act of 1963 enabled hereditary peers to relinquish their titles in order to sit in the House of Commons. It came about chiefly at the instigation of Labour's Anthony Wedgwood Benn – who was briefly the third Viscount Stansgate – but it also allowed the sudden elevation to Downing Street of the former Earl of Home (pronounced 'Hume').

A Scot like Macmillan, and the only prime minister to have played first-class cricket, Sir Alec was a laconic, cadaverous figure easy to parody in an age of declining deference – although his riposte to Harold Wilson's repeated references to his being the 14th Earl of Home was to murmur: 'I suppose Mr Wilson, when you come to think of it, is the 14th Mr Wilson.'

Home was chosen to replace Macmillan above more fancied candidates (particularly 'Rab' Butler), and showed his resilience by running Labour a close second in the 1964 election despite the fallout from the Profumo affair. Totally lacking in pomposity, he once artlessly confessed his weakness in economic matters by admitting, no doubt tongue in cheek, that 'I do my sums with matchsticks'.

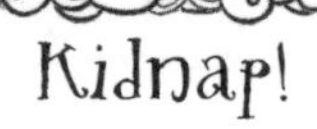

Kidnap!

In April 1964 two University of Aberdeen students attempted to kidnap the Prime Minister. Meeting them in public – and thinking it was a joke – he gave them a pound for charity. When they knocked on the door of the house where he was staying, however, Sir Alec realised they were serious.

Packing as if to leave with them, he poured them some beer and eventually persuaded them to abandon their plot. The clincher, it seems, was his forecast of the dire consequences should they take him away: 'If you do, the Conservatives will win the election by two or three hundred seats.'

Harold Wilson (Labour, 1964–1970 and 1974–1976). The squat, blunt Yorkshireman needed no matchsticks. After taking a first-class degree in Philosophy, Politics and Economics, he had become one of the youngest Oxford dons of the century, at just 21, and when appointed president of the Board of Trade ten years later he was the youngest cabinet minister of the 20th century.

In appearance dour and unimaginative, he nevertheless developed an ability to deliver punchy one-liners: 'No comment – in glorious Technicolor' was one reaction to the Profumo scandal. He approached the 1964 election as the champion of technological progress. 'The Britain that is going to be forged in the white heat of this revolution', he had declared at the Labour Party's annual conference, 'will be no place for restrictive practices or for outdated measures on either side of industry.'

Cloak and dagger

What hung over everything in these turbulent times was the dreadful image of a mushroom-shaped cloud. Whether anyone would dare to use them, nobody knew, but the Cold War adversaries bristled with nuclear weapons, and their leaders boasted of their readiness to press the button – if, they were always careful to say, the other side used them first.

In such an atmosphere the 'national security' panic regarding Christine Keeler, Profumo and Ivanov is at least understandable. Spies were thought to be everywhere...

• **George Blake**, a double agent working for the Soviet Union, betrayed some 400 MI6 agents to the Soviets. Arrested in 1961, he was given a prison sentence of 42 years, but he escaped from Wormwood Scrubs five years later and fled to the USSR.

• **John Vassall**, a homosexual, was working in the UK's Moscow embassy when he was plied with drink and photographed in compromising positions with several men. Blackmailed by the Soviets, he returned to Britain and handed over thousands of classified documents before being arrested in 1962 and sentenced to 18 years in gaol. He served ten of them.

• **Kim Philby.** After Donald Maclean and Guy Burgess had fled to Russia in the Fifties to avoid arrest, there were strong suspicions that Philby was 'the Third Man', but official bungling saved him. By 1963, however, it was clear that the net was closing around him, and he defected at night aboard a Soviet freighter.

The Cuban Missile Crisis

The world has never been closer to the horror of nuclear war than during a period of two nail-biting weeks in the autumn of 1962.

On 14 October a US Air Force U-2 spy plane captured photographic evidence that a Soviet missile base was under construction in Cuba. The Americans demanded that the site should be dismantled and all the weapons removed, but they decided on a military quarantine of the island rather than an immediate armed assault. Soviet president Nikita Krushchev responded with a bullish letter to President Kennedy, stating that the quarantine was 'an act of aggression propelling humankind into the abyss of a world nuclear-missile war'. They were eyeball to eyeball.

There were many who sympathised with the Cubans, who had resisted an armed invasion by the United States a year before at the Bay of Pigs, and for whom the Soviet Union was a friend in need. But few could witness the day-by-day nuclear stand-off with anything but mounting dread.

At last, on 28 October a secret deal was brokered by the United Nations secretary-general, U Thant. The Soviets would remove their weapons, and the Americans would never attempt to invade Cuba again.

The road from Aldermaston

The early Sixties were the heyday of the Aldermaston marches, held every Easter after the founding of the Campaign for Nuclear Disarmament (CND) in 1958. Here was a cause that divided the nation without ever achieving any decisive result. The campaigners, who spent days on the road marching down to London from the Atomic Weapons Research Establishment at Aldermaston in Berkshire, regarded Britain's possession of nuclear weapons as immoral. Their opponents regarded these bearded, sandalled hippies as out of touch with reality.

Tens of thousands trekked the 52-mile (83 km) route each year, the younger members of the host playing and singing their way along. John Brunner's 'The H-Bomb's Thunder' became the unofficial CND anthem, while other favourites included 'Brother Won't You Join the Line?', 'Doomsday Blues' and 'The Bomb Has Got to Go'.

The protests weren't confined to the Aldermaston event. In September 1961 the 89-year-old philosopher and life-long protester Bertrand Russell was jailed for a breach of the peace (that is, sitting down in Trafalgar Square and refusing to budge), and a few days later, at another ban-the-bomb demonstration, those arrested included the CND chairman Canon John Collins, the playwright John Osborne, the jazz musician George Melly and the actress Vanessa Redgrave.

The Berlin Wall

In the aftermath of the Second World War Winston Churchill made his famous speech describing a metaphorical 'iron curtain' dividing East from West. From 1961 the city of Berlin would be physically divided – at first by a stout fence and then, from 1965, by an impassable concrete wall with guard towers.

For East Germany this was the 'Anti-Fascist Protection Rampart', while for West Berlin's mayor (and later West German chancellor) Willy Brandt, it was the 'Wall of Shame'.

One of the grimmest legacies of the Cold War Sixties, it was finally demolished in 1989.

Winds of change

When he first said it, in Ghana in January 1960, nobody seemed to be listening – perhaps because the former Gold Coast already had its independence. But when Harold Macmillan repeated the phrase before South Africa's parliament in Cape Town three weeks later everyone sat up and took notice.

'The wind of change is blowing through this continent,' he told the MPs, 'and whether we like it or not, this growth of national consciousness is a political fact. We must all accept it as a fact, and our national policies must take account of it.'

This bold declaration of intent regarding the freedom of Britain's African possessions was anathema to the right wing of his own Conservative party at home, and the Monday Club pressure group was formed to fight it. *The Times* had obviously got the message loud and clear, however, for that April the paper quietly abandoned its section heading 'Imperial and Foreign News', replacing it with 'Overseas News'.

Decolonisation in Africa...

By the end of the 1960s, all Britain's African colonies except Southern Rhodesia (the future Zimbabwe) and the South African mandate of South West Africa (Namibia) had achieved independence.

Somalia 1960
Nigeria 1960
Sierra Leone 1961
Tanzania 1961
Uganda 1962
Kenya 1963
Malawi 1964
Zambia 1964
Gambia 1965
Botswana 1966
Lesotho 1966
Mauritius 1968
Swaziland 1968

...and elsewhere

Cyprus 1960
Jamaica 1962
Trinidad 1962
Malta 1964
Gozo 1964
British Honduras 1964
(Belize from 1973)
Barbados 1966
Guyana 1966

'Great Britain has lost an empire
and not yet found a role.'

Dean Acheson, former
US Secretary of State, in 1962

Another part of Macmillan's speech was unpopular with his local audience. 'As a fellow member of the Commonwealth,' he went on, 'it is our earnest desire to give South Africa our support and encouragement, but I hope you won't mind my saying frankly that there are some aspects of your policies which make it impossible for us to do this without being false to our own deep convictions about the political destinies of free men to which in our own territories we are trying to give effect.'

The following year, after a whites-only referendum, South Africa declared itself a republic and left the Commonwealth. Its racist *apartheid* policy would make it an international pariah until the 1990s.

There remained the problem of Southern Rhodesia which, likewise, would not be resolved for many years (it finally became Zimbabwe in 1980). The British government refused to grant the country independence without majority rule, and the response of Ian Smith's white-dominated government was to make a unilateral declaration of independence (UDI) in November 1965.

UDI was condemned by the international community, and – at Britain's request – the United Nations authorised economic sanctions. The following year Harold Wilson made one last effort to reach a deal with Smith, the two men having secret meetings aboard the cruiser HMS *Tiger* off Gibraltar, but the gulf between them proved to be too great.

Mourning the president

The assassination of US president John F. Kennedy on 22 November 1963 was more than a shock to the British people: it felt almost like a personal bereavement.

In those troubled and changing times, his youthful charisma seemed to speak to the idealism of a generation grown weary with the platitudes of politicians mired in the past.

People queued in their thousands to record their loss in books of remembrance, and the usually iconoclastic *TW3* ditched its satire and created a tribute programme instead.

Vietnam

The US conflict in Vietnam, like the Iraq war decades later, sharply divided public opinion in the West, and there were mass protests on both sides of the Atlantic.

Harold Wilson repeatedly refused requests to involve British troops in the war – causing a strained relationship with US president Lyndon B. Johnson.

In March 1968 some 10,000 protestors gathered in London's Trafalgar Square before marching to the American embassy in Grosvenor Square. The actress Vanessa Redgrave was allowed to enter the embassy to deliver a letter of protest, but more than 200 people were arrested after violent clashes with mounted police.

The following October 25,000 anti-war demonstrators marched on the embassy once again, but a force of a thousand police officers restrained them.

In November the American journalist Seymour Hersh broke the story of the My Lai atrocity, in which more than 500 innocent South Vietnamese civilians were massacred in their village by a US platoon.

Closer to home

The racial tolerance Britain preached abroad was soon to be put to the test at home. It had been enshrined in the 1965 Race Relations Act, one of a series of liberal laws introduced by Wilson's Labour government (see pages 28–29), and a refinement was set to come onto the statute books in 1968.

The early Sixties had seen a steady influx from Commonwealth countries. Although the shameful 'No blacks, no dogs, no Irish' letting boards were a thing of the past, immigrant families were still often pushed to the back of the queue for housing and jobs. This discrimination would now be outlawed.

At this very moment, however, the home secretary, James Callaghan, introduced legislation to Parliament precisely designed to keep large numbers of African Asians out of the country. These were the victims of aggressive pro-black policies being pursued in Kenya and Uganda, two countries which had recently achieved their independence.

With a thousand Asians a month arriving in Britain, Callaghan devised his Commonwealth Immigrants Bill which, overnight, made their UK passports invalid. A limited number of 'special vouchers' would be issued instead.

He dismissed (in a memo) the argument that emigration from the country usefully offset the numbers arriving: 'This view overlooks the important point that emigration is largely by white persons from nearly every corner of the United Kingdom, while immigration and settlement are largely by coloured persons into a relatively small number of concentrated areas. The exchange thus aggravates rather than alleviates the problem.'

The foaming Tiber

The bill had many critics, including notable Conservative figures such as Iain Macleod, Ian Gilmour and Michael Heseltine, and it must have been a great relief to Callaghan when someone else came along to take the flak. This was the shadow foreign secretary Enoch Powell, who made a notorious speech in Birmingham on 20 April 1968.

'As I look ahead,' he intoned, 'I am filled with foreboding. Like the Roman, I seem to see "the River Tiber foaming with much blood".' (Powell was a classicist, and 'the Roman' was the ancient poet Virgil.) He also quoted one of his Wolverhampton constituents, who had told him that 'In this country in 15 or 20 years' time the black man will have the whip hand over the white man.'

It was described by *The Times* as 'an evil speech'. Tory leader Edward Heath promptly fired Powell from the shadow cabinet.

Two American deaths

In his 'Rivers of Blood' speech (as it came to be called) Enoch Powell mentioned 'that tragic and intractable phenomenon which we watch with horror on the other side of the Atlantic'. He was referring to the race riots which had spread to more than a hundred US cities after the assassination of the civil rights leader Martin Luther King in Memphis on 4 April.

The American people were soon to be shocked by yet another killing. Senator Robert Kennedy, himself a staunch supporter of minority rights, was shot dead in Los Angeles on 2 June.

Many supported Powell, though. A thousand London dockers went on strike to protest about his sacking, marching on Parliament with placards which read DON'T KNOCK ENOCH and BACK BRITAIN, NOT BLACK BRITAIN. They lobbied the Labour MPs Peter Shore and Ian Mikardo, who was kicked. When Lady Gaitskell, widow of the former Labour leader, shouted that they would have their remedy at the next election, some replied: 'We won't forget.' They probably didn't.

I'm Backing Britain

A strange campaign with this slogan was launched in 1968 when five secretaries from Surbiton offered to work an extra half an hour each day without pay to boost productivity.

Within a week their cause had taken off nationally, Harold Wilson had given it his support and the campaign's Union Flag logo could be seen in every high street. The newspaper tycoon Robert Maxwell suggested adding a 'Buy British' element, although the campaign's T-shirts were made in Portugal.

In a very British way it all fizzled out within a few months, having had no effect whatsoever.

That was 1968 that was

The recent flowers-in-your hair Summer of Love must have seemed long forgotten among the worldwide political upheavals which occurred in this single remarkable year.

In China Mao Tse-Tung had a firm grip on his Cultural Revolution, but elsewhere in the Communist bloc there were student protests in Yugoslavia and Poland, while Soviet troops poured into Czechoslovakia during the 'Prague Spring' to overthrow Alexander Dubček's popular reformist government.

Elsewhere there were sit-ins, marches and demonstrations – often led by students, often violently put down – about civil rights, the Vietnam war and a host of local issues, from Japan to Europe, from the US and Canada to Jamaica, Mexico and Brazil.

In France agitation for university reform (there were a few tame occupations of UK universities, too) escalated into a violent outpouring of dissatisfaction with the old regime, and to a crippling national strike.

The French, of course, philosophised about the phenomenon, but if their 'revolution' came to nothing it was surely because those at the barricades knew more about what they were against than what they were for.

The Troubles

The so-called Troubles in Northern Ireland are usually reckoned to date from October 1968, when activists defied a government ban on their civil rights march in Belfast and were attacked by the Royal Ulster Constabulary, leading to three days of rioting.

Violence escalated throughout the last year of the decade. That April the Roman Catholic Bernadette Devlin became the youngest woman ever elected to the British Parliament (the record still stands as of 2012). A few days later the Ministry of Defence sent army reinforcements into the province for the first time since the Second World War.

In August, with eight people shot dead, more than a hundred treated for gunshot wounds and Protestants setting fire to hundreds of homes in Catholic areas of Belfast, the British army was deployed on the streets. The soldiers would stay there for 38 years.

Grey heat

Although his government reduced the voting age from 21 to 18 and passed several laws reflecting the relaxed moral code of the time, Harold Wilson's image is less that of a free spirit riding the Sixties breeze than a cautious manipulator forever watching his back.

Modernisation was the theme of his 1964 election campaign, but the 'white heat' of his planned technological revolution turned out to be rather grey. There was to be no place for restrictive practices in industry, yet ministers seemed to spend a great many valuable hours in proverbial (and actual) smoke-filled rooms, finessing deals with uppity union leaders over sandwiches and mugs of thick brown tea.

Adroit at playing left against right in his own party, Wilson managed the considerable feat of converting Labour to the idea of joining the Common Market – only for French president General de Gaulle to veto Britain's application, just as he had a few years earlier when Harold Macmillan first tried to get through the door.

And yet Wilson's government *did* get quite a lot done. For good or ill, Britain was a very different place at the end of the Sixties from what it had been at the beginning.

> 'This party is a moral crusade
> or it is nothing.'
>
> *Harold Wilson on Labour*

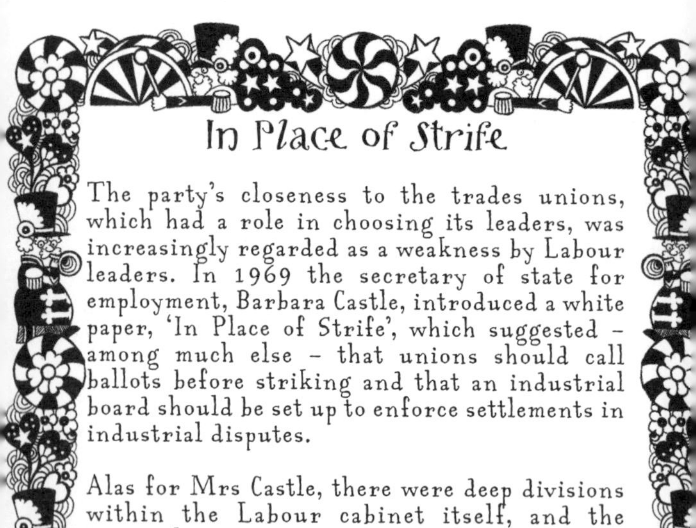

In Place of Strife

The party's closeness to the trades unions, which had a role in choosing its leaders, was increasingly regarded as a weakness by Labour leaders. In 1969 the secretary of state for employment, Barbara Castle, introduced a white paper, 'In Place of Strife', which suggested – among much else – that unions should call ballots before striking and that an industrial board should be set up to enforce settlements in industrial disputes.

Alas for Mrs Castle, there were deep divisions within the Labour cabinet itself, and the proposals were dropped.

The Open University

The jury is still out on Labour's drive to turn grammar schools into comprehensives, but few would disagree that one of the party's greatest legacies (driven through by the arts minister, Jennie Lee) was the Open University.

The new university would accept students without any previous qualifications, and they would study at home rather than on campus. The Tory MP Iain Macleod thought the idea 'blithering nonsense', but the playwright Willy Russell later acknowledged the value of this 'higher education for all' institution: his 1980 comedy *Educating Rita* is set in the office of an Open University lecturer, and Rita and her tutor both find their lives transformed by the OU experience.

As for conventional universities, Labour continued the expansion begun by the Conservatives, a total of 23 being founded during the decade.

The new universities

1961	University of Sussex
1962	Keele University
1963	University of East Anglia University of York Newcastle University
1964	University of Strathclyde Lancaster University
1965	University of Kent University of Essex University of Warwick
1966	Loughborough University Aston University Brunel University University of Surrey University of Bath University of Bradford City University, London Heriot-Watt University
1967	University of Salford University of Dundee University of Stirling Royal College of Art
1969	Cranfield University

The Beeching axe

A less happy episode was the modernisation (or 'reshaping') of the country's railway system carried out by Dr Richard Beeching – commonly known as the 'Beeching axe'.

His view was that the losses experienced by British Railways since the 1950s would grow even more severe without drastic action, and that meant closing lines all over the country. Within ten years of his report more than 4,000 miles (6,400 km) of railway and all of 3,000 stations had disappeared – 25 per cent of all route miles and 50 per cent of stations.

Beeching's name, widely reviled today, lives on in a number of places where the railway once ran, including his own home town of East Grinstead in Sussex. The A22 relief road through the town descends into a deep cutting which was originally made for the railway line. The locals, not surprisingly, wanted to name this section of road Beeching Cut, but the authorities thought this was rather too pointed, and today you drive along Beeching Way instead.

Blots on the landscape

It wasn't only the moral and cultural landscape that changed during the Sixties. To live in a large town was to witness the physical landscape being transformed by the intrusion of large, concrete, squared-off office blocks – a sign of growing prosperity, no doubt, but also of developers being allowed to get away (or so it seemed to the dazed onlooker) with practically anything they liked.

Cathy Come Home

While property developers were throwing up new headquarters for businesses, many families had trouble finding a decent place to live. The problem of homelessness was highlighted in the BBC play *Cathy Come Home*, which shocked the nation.

Written by Jeremy Sandford, it told the story of a woman who, after her husband loses his job because of injury, has her children taken away by social services.

Twelve million viewers tuned in, and a new awareness of the housing crisis gave a shot in the arm to the newly formed charity, Shelter.

Perhaps the architects were paying tribute to such giants of their profession as Frank Lloyd Wright and Le Corbusier – but the resulting 'Brutalist' style is largely unloved today.

Along came a group of stained-glass students from the Royal College of Art who called themselves Anti-Ugly Action. When the first stone was laid for Barclays Bank's new headquarters in London, they placed a black coffin on the pavement outside, bearing the epitaph 'Here lyeth British architecture.' Cards were issued to members of the public so that they could recommend buildings for 'the Anti-Ugly seal of disapproval'. Regular protests followed.

It was all good fun, of course, but the sudden rash of unlovely buildings was something of a mystery. Why was there so much ugliness up in the sky while, down at street level in the boutiques, accessory shops and even in the car factories, the country was awash with dazzling, original design?

‘Nothing happened in the Sixties except that we all dressed up.’

John Lennon

‘Fashion is not frivolous. It is a part of being alive today.’

Mary Quant

Chapter Three

Dedicated Followers of Fashion

In April 1966 America's *Time* magazine devoted one of its famous covers to 'swinging' London – 'a city steeped in tradition, seized by change, liberated by affluence'.

The cartoonish medley of images combined the old (Big Ben, 'bobbies', red double-decker buses, city gents in Rolls-Royces) with the new (discos, miniskirts, rock stars, dolly birds, casinos and bingo halls, E-type Jags and Mini Coopers), while the article inside trumpeted the notion that 'In a once sedate world of faded splendor, everything new, uninhibited and kinky is blooming at the top of London life.'

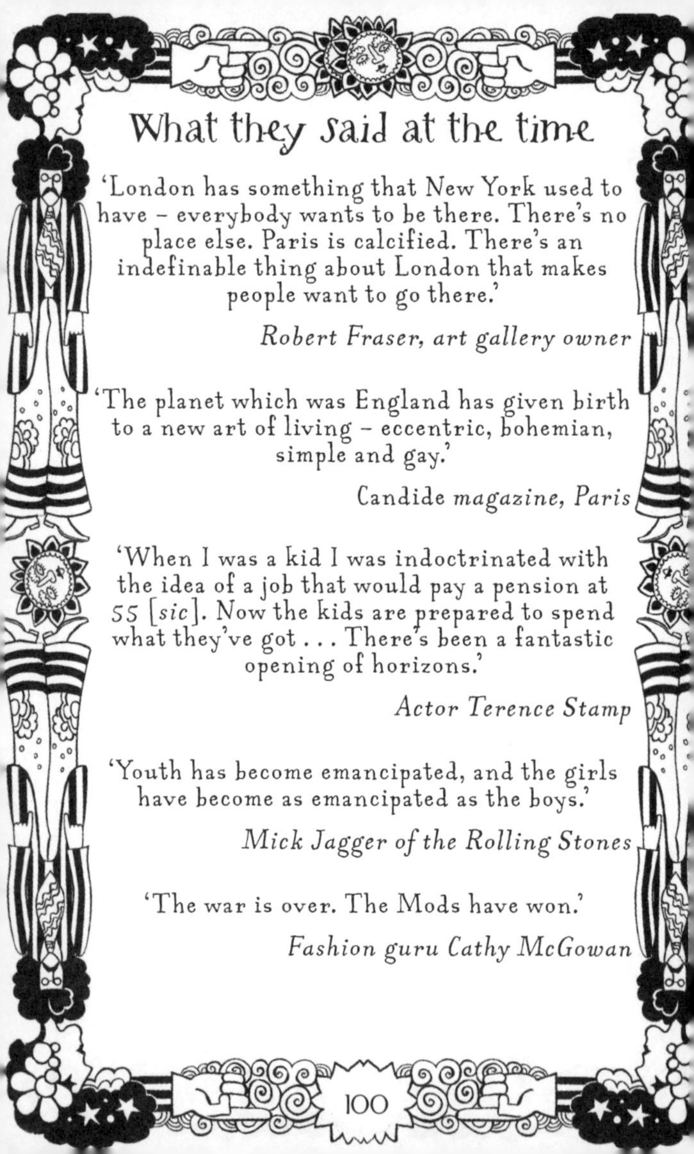

What they said at the time

'London has something that New York used to have – everybody wants to be there. There's no place else. Paris is calcified. There's an indefinable thing about London that makes people want to go there.'

Robert Fraser, art gallery owner

'The planet which was England has given birth to a new art of living – eccentric, bohemian, simple and gay.'

Candide *magazine, Paris*

'When I was a kid I was indoctrinated with the idea of a job that would pay a pension at 55 [*sic*]. Now the kids are prepared to spend what they've got . . . There's been a fantastic opening of horizons.'

Actor Terence Stamp

'Youth has become emancipated, and the girls have become as emancipated as the boys.'

Mick Jagger of the Rolling Stones

'The war is over. The Mods have won.'

Fashion guru Cathy McGowan

Roger Miller's limp contemporary ballad 'England Swings (Like a Pendulum Do)' chose to highlight the traditional – eulogising the supposed 'rosy red cheeks of the little children' – but it was the sassy, dynamic, cash-fuelled outburst of colour and style that startled any visitor to mid-Sixties London and, thanks to a rapid osmosis, Britain as a whole.

At the wheel of this gaudy charabanc were the baby-boomers, a teeming generation of youngsters conceived in the aftermath of the war and now suddenly revelling in a new prosperity. Jobs were plentiful – you could walk out of one in the afternoon and pick up another in the morning – and the idea of saving for a rainy day was little short of pitiful.

Carnaby Street and the King's Road in London were suddenly the fashion epicentre for every style-conscious youngster – the 'pretty flamingo' of the Manfred Mann song, the 'dedicated follower of fashion' parodied by the Kinks. These were the well-groomed Mods we've already seen engaged in fisticuffs with greasy Rockers at the seaside, and it was their culture which now came out on top.

Revving up

Lambretta and Vespa scooters were the ubiquitous Mod means of transport, but owning a car became more and more feasible as the decade lengthened. Only the most prosperous could afford a sleek E-type Jaguar, but that other motoring icon of the Sixties, the Mini, was everyone's favourite – even if its front-mounted engine proved so liable to flooding in wet weather that many an owner placed a sheet of cardboard behind the radiator grille to protect it.

The World Cup

As if conquering the worlds of fashion and pop music weren't enough, swinging Britain added an improbable sports trophy to its cupboard in July 1966 when England's footballers beat West Germany at Wembley to win the World Cup for the only time in their history.

The victory owed a great deal to the distinctly old-fashioned grit of players such as Nobby Stiles and Jack Charlton (not to speak of a questionable decision by a Russian linesman), but the euphoria which greeted it was all part of the 60s' spirit of carefree rejuvenation.

Designed by Alec Issigonis in response to petrol rationing after the 1956 Suez crisis, the Mini was launched in 1959, had notched up sales of a million by 1965, and eventually became the best-selling British car in history, with a production run of 5.3 million by the time it was discontinued in 2000.

It was a sporting sensation, too. In 1964 Paddy Hopkirk drove one to victory in the Monte Carlo rally, and the Finnish driver Timo Mäkinen repeated the performance the following year when only 35 out of 237 cars reached the finishing line in atrocious conditions – three of them being Minis.

One gloriously daft pastime was cramming as many people as possible into the car, with scores of above twenty commonplace. (They mercifully didn't take to the road with this payload.) The practice has continued with the evolution of the car into the rather larger BMW Mini, and in January 2011 the Pilobolus dance company entered the *Guinness Book of Records* when the doors were closed – with some difficulty – on no fewer than 26 of their slim and lycra-clad members.

Top gear

What were the Sixties young things wearing? By its very nature fashion is fickle (the Kinks' popinjay could be seen one week in polka-dots, the next in stripes), but here's a range of popular Mod clothes and accessories around the middle of the decade.

For her:

- **Miniskirts and A-line minidresses, the hemline several inches above the knee**
- **Chiffon baby-doll dresses and shift dresses**
- **Tights, often patterned (it was their invention which made the wearing of miniskirts possible)**
- **White, knee-high go-go boots**
- **Beehive hairdos**
- **False eyelashes and kohl eyeliner**
- **Short plastic raincoats on top**
- **Bikinis for the beach.**

'It's a bad joke that won't last – not with winter coming.'

Designer Coco Chanel on the miniskirt, 1966

For him:

- 'City gent' look, with tailored suits and button-down shirt collars
- Slim ties
- Tight, tapered trousers
- Levi jeans for casual wear
- Winkle-picker shoes
- Short, neat hair, often 'bowl-style' as sported by Brian Jones of the Rolling Stones
- Anoraks on top when out on the scooter.

A taxing problem

Rapidly rising hemlines raised eyebrows and temperatures everywhere, but they were a special worry for the Inland Revenue.

Any dress less than 24 inches (61 cm) long was classed as children's clothing and was therefore free of tax – but now mature women were proudly flaunting their thighs in garments that had been designed with youngsters in mind.

The taxman, as ever, found a remedy. From 1 January 1966 women's clothes were assessed according to their bust size rather than their length.

Something from nothing

Sixties fashion designers were nothing if not inventive:

- John Stephen, 'the king of Carnaby Street', had the bright idea of turning a mohair rug into a pullover, and Cliff Richard wore it to appear on BBC's *Top of the Pops* programme the very next day.
- In 1967 Paul Reeves and his business partner Pete Sutch bought several Indian bedcovers from a Kensington department store and turned them into full-length kaftans complete with Nehru collars and half-belts at the back. Mick Jagger and George Harrison bought a couple in Chelsea antiques market, and they went on to become a major fashion craze.

By the late Sixties the hippie movement had inspired a more casual style for both sexes – flares, bell-bottom jeans, peasant shirts and blouses, T-shirts, bandanas and floral scarves. Hair was grown longer, and you would indeed sometimes see a flower in it.

fashion icons

All this colourful primping and preening made household names of certain enterprising individuals who seized the moment to stamp their own mark on the rampant couturial world about them.

The Welsh fashion designer Mary Quant, who opened her first Bazaar boutique in Chelsea as long ago as 1955 and followed it with a second in Knightsbridge six years later, is generally credited with inventing the miniskirt – although the French designer André Courrèges also laid claim to the achievement.

Born in 1934, Quant was older than most of her clients, but she was such a dynamic trendsetter that she was awarded an OBE as early as 1966. (She arrived at Buckingham Palace to receive her award in a micro-miniskirt and black cutaway gloves.)

A girl dressed by Quant might be seen, as the mood took her, in hotpants (she devised those, too), a sweater dress with plastic collar, a balloon-style dress or knickerbockers over brightly patterned stretch stockings. The designer's knee-length lace-up boots in white plastic, together with plastic raincoats, became part of the 'London Look'.

One thing you might prefer *not* to know about Mary Quant: up above she sported a short, bobbed hairstyle which became all the rage, but down below she shaved her pubic hair into a heart shape – and dyed it green.

Barbara Hulanicki, only a little younger than Quant, launched her clothes store Biba in Kensington in 1964, and pop stars, film stars and would-be stars flocked to it. Its vibrant interior was inspired by Art Deco and Art Nouveau. Here you could buy unisex T-shirts in rich, dark colours, velvet trouser suits, floppy felt hats and even feather boas.

Hulanicki made her own claim about the miniskirt. Soon after her store opened, she said, she rather desperately put on the shelves a consignment of skirts in stretchy jersey fabric which had shrunk drastically in transit and were only 10 inches (25 cm) long: 'God, I thought, we'll go bust – we'll never be able to sell them. I couldn't sleep, but that little fluted skirt walked out on customers as fast as we could get it onto the hatstands.' (Antique hatstands were a distinctive feature of the shop's displays.)

When the Victoria and Albert Museum displayed her designs years later, it gave a pen portrait of 'the classic Biba dolly', who was young and very pretty:

'She had an upturned nose, rosy cheeks and a skinny body with long asparagus legs and tiny feet.

'She was square-shouldered and quite flat-chested. Her head was perched on a long, swan-like neck. Her face was a perfect oval, her lids were heavy with long, spiky lashes. She looked sweet but was as hard as nails. She did what she felt like at that moment and had no mum to influence her judgement.'

This romantic view caught an essential point about the young clientele. Most of them certainly weren't orphans, but they were shopping with an abandon their mothers could only have dreamed of, and choosing styles that, with a few brave exceptions, only their own generation would think of wearing.

Imagine, for instance, tripping out in a dress with flashing lighbulbs down the front. This was the creation of Ossie Clark for his 1965 degree show at the Royal College of Art, and it was splashed across newspapers and fashion magazines everywhere.

Clark became synonymous with Sixties Op Art flair, and collaborated with Alice Pollock to create dresses for her exclusive King's Road boutique Quorum, working in collaboration with Celia Birtwell, who produced textiles and designed scintillating prints. Clark and Birtwell eventually married, and sat for one of David Hockney's most famous portraits, *Mr and Mrs Clark and Percy* (1970).

By 1967 there were two thousand boutiques in the Greater London area – and they weren't only catering for the girls. For their fathers a (rare) night out meant putting on a smart suit and a tie, but the young men of the Sixties generation expected to flock to the nightspots looking every bit as striking as their dates.

Pretty faces

Models aplenty were required to show off the inventive designs of the period, but two stood out in Sixties Britain.

• **The Shrimp**
Jean Shrimpton, born in November 1942, had undeniable beauty. Doe-eyed and pouty, slim and long-legged, she appeared on the covers of every fashionable magazine. She had affairs with the photographer David Bailey and the actor Terence Stamp before marrying another photographer, Michael Cox.

• **Twiggy**
Lesley Hornby's modelling name was no exaggeration. Born in September 1949, she was 5 ft 6 in (1.68 m) tall but weighed a mere 8 stone (51 kg). Some critics thought her thinness unhealthy, though in fact it was her natural build. Her early career was managed by her then boyfriend, the hairdresser Nigel Davies, who restyled himself Justin de Villeneuve. Her hair was cut in a short, boyish style, her eyelids fluttered dark (multi-layered) lashes and her stick figure was ideal for the androgynous A-line dresses of the period.

She retired from modelling in 1970, saying that she couldn't spend her life being 'a coat-hanger', but she returned to it in her maturity and was still in front of the cameras as this book went to press.

The London guru of men's fashion was John Stephen. A grocer's son from Glasgow, he opened his first boutique in 1963 and at one time owned more than a dozen of them in Carnaby Street alone, as well as branches in the United States, Italy and Norway. Although he always dressed in traditional fashion himself, he knew exactly what his young clientele wanted.

His stores (he soon catered for women, too) were crammed with his own creations and loud to the beat of rock music – fittingly, since groups such as the Beatles, the Rolling Stones, the Bee Gees and the Kinks were regular customers.

A few of his triumphs, major and minor:

- **He imported the first pair of Levis into the UK, and they were an instant success.**

- **The singer Petula Clark and pianist Liberace filmed one of their TV spectaculars in one of his Carnaby Street shops.**

- **He was so successful that he bought the first of his many Rolls-Royces at the age of 20.**

But what if you lived far from the bright lights of London? Not to worry, because there were chain stores throughout the country (Chelsea Girl, Bus Stop, Miss Selfridge) offering the latest fashions at affordable prices.

There had been, that *Time* cover piece trumpeted brazenly, 'a bloodless revolution'. It quoted the sociologist Richard Hoggart ('a slum orphan', it reminded its readers) to the effect that a new group was emerging into society, 'creating a kind of classlessness and a verve which has not been seen before'.

Ready, steady, McGowan

In a typical Sixties rise to fame, Cathy McGowan, who formerly worked in the fashion department of *Women's Own* magazine, was chosen as the face of 'the typical teenager' by the Friday night Rediffusion TV programme *Ready Steady Go!* (slogan: 'The weekend starts here!') and soon became its regular presenter. The fact that she regularly mangled her lines didn't matter. She had style – becoming known as the 'Queen of the Mods' – and she was down to earth. Twiggy later said: 'I'd sit and drool over her clothes. She was a heroine to us because she was one of us.'

Watch the birdie

This was a wild exaggeration, of course, but the age certainly threw up a host of celebrities who boasted humble beginnings (yes, you *could* brag about that now) and yet mingled easily with the 'nobs'. This was nowhere better exemplified than in the world of fashion photography, where Patrick Lichfield, who inherited an earldom in 1960, and Anthony Armstrong-Jones, who married Princess Margaret and became the Earl of Snowdon, were joined by a bevy of up-and-comers from the working class.

The most famous of them was David Bailey, who bought his first Rolleiflex camera on being demobbed from the army in 1958 and within two years was working for *Vogue* magazine. His *Box of Pin-Ups*, brought out in 1964, contained prints of celebrities such as the model Jean Shrimpton (his lover), the Beatles, Mick Jagger, Terence Stamp, Rudolf Nureyev, Andy Warhol and those notorious East End gangsters, the Kray twins – their inclusion in this Sixties pantheon occasioning an angry outburst from Lord Snowdon.

Bailey was both attractive and energetic, with a dangerous edge. Married four times (one of his wives was the actress Catherine Deneuve), he found the stars practically queuing up to be captured by his lens.

Something unlikely about David Bailey: he once shared his house with sixty parrots – and contracted psittacosis.

Blow-Up

David Hemmings, Vanessa Redgrave, Sarah Miles and Jane Birkin were among the star-studded cast of Michelangelo Antonioni's quintessential Sixties film *Blow-Up*. The story of a photographer who suspects he has witnessed a murder, it was partly inspired by the life of David Bailey.

Because of its explicit content (*Premiere* magazine termed one scene 'the sexiest cinematic moment in history'), it was refused approval in the USA. MGM's decision to go ahead and release it anyway had the effect of changing the US rating system to match the more relaxed times.

Terence Donovan, born in the East End of London in 1936, took his first photograph at the age of 15 and used local bomb sites as a backdrop for his original work. His early 'photo-essays' documented the seedier underbelly of London life, but by the mid-Sixties he had become a regular contributor to *Vogue* and *Harper's Bazaar* – and, of course, a regular on the celebrity circuit, mingling with artists, rock singers, actors and actresses.

He was no flatterer, however, and Cecil Beaton, one of the old school, recognised that something had changed: 'Donovan's young girls', he said later, 'had no innocence and he somehow contrived to make them look as if they were wearing soiled underwear.'

Norman Parkinson, another old-timer, described Bailey, Donovan and Brian Duffy – the third star in the Sixties photographic firmament – as a 'black trinity'. Duffy had his own riposte to that kind of put-down: 'Before us,' he said, 'fashion photographers were tall, thin and camp. We're different. We're short, fat and heterosexual.'

Cut and bob

This new world of unashamed dash and display made stars of hairdressers, too, although 'Teasy Weasy' Raymond began the decade with his Mayfair salon already famous. In 1956 he had been flown to the United States merely to cut the hair of the film star Diana Dors (for the price of a small house in Britain), and in 1968 he would perform a similar service for another actress, Mia Farrow, for a cool $5,000.

Jackie lends a hand

What every young girl needed in the turbulent Sixties was advice about growing up in a world whose rules were rapidly changing. In 1964 along came *Jackie* magazine with a 'Cathy and Claire' problem page which handled 400 letters every week. It immediately sold 350,000 copies a week, and the circulation rose steadily.

Most of the letters were about sex, but the Scottish publishers didn't feel the time was yet ripe for explicitness about such matters in the public prints. What they did was create a series of leaflets covering the main areas of concern, and they sent these out in reply.

Born Raymondo Bessone to Italian parents in Brixton, south London, in 1911, Raymond started his working life by making false beards and moustaches in his father's barber shop. By the time he had become the nation's first celebrity hairdresser he had transformed himself into a camp figure with a fake French accent, his salon fitted out with gilt mirrors, chandeliers and champagne fountains.

Spend, spend, spend!

One of the saddest sagas of the Sixties (some regarded it as a morality tale) was the huge football-pools win in 1961 by the penniless Yorkshire couple Keith and Vivian Nicholson and its unedifying aftermath. Viv was determined to splash the cash as ostentatiously as she could – a pink Cadillac was but one indulgence among many – and her declared motto was 'Spend, spend, spend!'

By the time Keith died at the wheel of his Jaguar four years later they had got through it all. A musical based on her life opened in 1998 and had a run in London's West End.

Credited with being the originator of the bouffant hair style, he was the first hairdresser to appear on television, and he had his own Saturday afternoon show during the Sixties.

Teasy Weasy was secretive about his cutting techniques, but one man who worked under him picked up enough of them to become the biggest name of all. Vidal Sassoon broke into the new barriers-down world of the time in similar fashion to that 'black trinity' of working-class photographers. Brought up in poverty in Shepherds Bush, west London, and spending years in a Jewish orphanage, he discovered a talent that gave him star status – and made him wealthy.

Sassoon created the first worldwide chain of hairdressing salons and made a fortune from his hair-treatment products. While Teasy Weasy looked back to a glamorous age of extravagant film-star hairdos, his protégé revolutionised the cutting business, creating simple but striking styles for the Mods. His 'wash and wear', low-maintenance philosophy did away with the need for lacquer sprays to keep the hair in place, releasing women from the tyranny of a regular shampoo-and-set. Sassoon typically cut hair short and into geometric shapes, relying on its natural shine to achieve what lacquer had done before, and in 1963 he created the classic 'bob cut' – angular and on a horizontal plane. Another of his styles, originally created for models showing off a Mary Quant collection, became known as the Nancy Kwan cut, after the Eurasian-American actress who first sported it in a *Vogue* photoshoot by Terence Donovan.

Doc Martens

They hardly suited every Mod style, but we should give a nod in the direction of Doc Martens, which were born in an earlier age but were first launched in the UK on 1 April 1960 – and have never gone away.

The German army doctor Klaus Martens invented the boots after damaging an ankle in a 1945 skiing accident and finding nothing on the market sufficiently comfortable.

When they at last arrived in Britain they were popular among postmen, police officers and factory workers – and would later become a fashion statement for Seventies skinheads.

Habitat

The exciting new life on the streets and in the nightclubs was matched by a burst of colourful stylishness in the home, and the star of this expanding domestic firmament was Terence Conran.

There's no better indicator of the changing times than the explanation he gave for the success of his first Habitat store, opened in the Fulham Road, Chelsea, in 1964: it was, he said, one of the few places where you could buy cheap pasta storage jars just at the moment when dried pasta was appearing in kitchens all over Britain.

Conran wasn't a working-class lad made good. The son of a businessman, he'd been privately educated at Bryanston school in Dorset before studying textiles at the Central Saint Martins college of art and design in London, working for a firm of architects, and then starting his own design practice. (He created a shop for Mary Quant.) His philosophy, he said, was 'plain, simple and useful', and his target customer was someone on a teacher's salary.

It was chiefly as a vehicle for his own Summa range of furniture that he opened that first Habitat, and there were soon branches throughout the country with the same trademark quarry-tiled floors, whitewashed brick walls, wood-slatted ceilings and spotlights, the merchandise stacked on the shelves as in a warehouse.

In these bright emporiums 'baby-boomers' with cash in their pockets discovered how to express themselves at home through a range of fabrics and furnishings their postwar parents could never have imagined seeing in the shops, let alone being able to afford.

On trend

Time *magazine offered this guide to the argot of Swinging London in 1966:*

'Talking the flip jargon that has become basic English for teenagers, jet setters and indeed any knowledgeable adult striving to maintain the illusion that he is at least young in heart, the switched-on London bird or beatle calls his urb "super", "fab", "groovy", "gear", "close" or "with it".'

What every home needed

It was fun setting up home in the Sixties, because there were so many new things to buy:

- **Lava lamps.** They weren't much good as lighting, but their introduction in 1963 gave everyone's sitting room a 'talking point'.

- **Glass-topped coffee tables.** It was the clean-cut look which appealed, however impractical they proved to be.

- **Goatskin rugs.** Foreign travel encouraged many a fad. These were fine if you didn't trip over them – and if they didn't get wet.

- **Futons.** Another foreign import, and very trendy. Ideal for latecomers who needed somewhere to crash.

- **Japanese paper lanterns.** Fly traps, of course, but they seemed indescribably elegant.

- **Bean bags.** In bright colours, and wonderful to snuggle down into.

- **Inflatable plastic chairs.** Equally colourful – but not quite so comfortable!

The Great Train Robbery

In the early hours of 8 August 1963 a Royal Mail train on its way from Glasgow to London was stopped by a hooded gang some 15 strong dressed in blue boiler suits. The driver, Jack Mills, was badly beaten, and the men got away with £2.6 million in banknotes – worth something like £40 million today.

The Great Train Robbery became the stuff of legend, books and films, though admiration for the audacity of the operation was compromised by its (unplanned) violence.

Within months most of the gang had been caught – several were given 30-year prison sentences – and although only about £400,000 was ever recovered, much of their haul was lost, spent on lawyers' fees or used to pay off underworld contacts.

Ronnie Biggs, who played a minor role in the robbery, became famous after escaping from Wandsworth prison to enjoy years of freedom, first in Australia and then in Brazil. He returned to Britain voluntarily in 2001 and was ordered to serve the rest of his sentence, but he was released on compassionate grounds eight years later because of ill health.

For Habitat's customers it was goodbye to dark, heavy wooden sideboards, three-piece suites, floral carpets and willow-patterned china, and welcome to a fresher, cleaner look: plastic mugs and storage cubes in vibrant colours, rustic French cookware, modular shelving, pine floors, Scandinavian furniture.

And, fittingly for a store that was part of Swinging London, its early customers included stars such as the actress Julie Christie and Beatles John Lennon and George Harrison, while Mary Quant not only designed the staff's outfits but bought complete settings of Habitat linen, glassware and crockery for her dinner parties.

DIY

Why were the young so keen to create modern nests for themselves? Because they were marrying at what now seems a very early age – an average of around 23 for men and 21 for women – and having children very soon afterwards. Many of those who wore the latest fashions and danced to the latest rhythms were home-builders, too. They found that the new relaxed spirit of the age had also affected bank managers: no longer stern upholders of fiscal chastity, these former pillars of rectitude were now willing to bestow their favours on anyone who could make a decent case for a mortgage.

The surprised new home-owners not only decked out their rooms with modern furniture and the latest gadgets, but busily changed the very fabric if it failed to suit their style.

Not the way to do it!

By far the *least* fashionable character in these pages is Barry Bucknell, the BBC's rolled-shirt-sleeved do-it-yourself expert. He worked under a severe handicap: his TV programme went out live, accidents and all. On one occasion, struck by a length of freshly glued wallpaper, he had to admit: 'That's how *not* to do it.'

His 1962 series *Bucknell's House* showed viewers how to modernise older properties by getting rid of clutter 'to introduce clear, modern lines'. This meant ripping out period features or covering them with plywood, and the amiable broadcaster is now remembered for promoting cultural vandalism.

What they ate at the time

A restaurant meal in the Sixties offered much less choice than today. A young couple pushing the boat out for a special occasion might have chosen from the following, to the soothing accompaniment of a dinner-jacketed pianist:

Aperitif
- A Babycham or vodka and lime for her; a lager for him

Starter
- Prawn cocktail in Marie Rose sauce
- Avocado with prawns

Main course
- Quiche lorraine (the very first quiche to reach Britain, it seemed very swish)
- Duck à l'orange (again, what sophistication!)
- Beef bourgignon

Dessert
- Black Forest gâteau from the sweet trolley

Wine
- White: German Riesling, Liebfraumilch or Blue Nun; Graves or Mâcon from France
- Red: Médoc or St-Emilion
- Rosé: Mateus Rosé from Portugal

Afterwards
- Gaelic coffee and mints.

Out with the old

A house-building boom provided a rash of new starter homes, many of them poorly constructed but nevertheless catering for the taste of the time: well lit, open plan, pine boards and so on. Older buildings, on the other hand, often seemed dark and pokey, and their occupants set about stripping and remodelling with a ruthlessness which has left its mark half a century later.

In days when it was still possible for the mechanically minded to get under a car and fix the engine, tampering with walls, chimneys and staircases seemed a straightforward task; it often made good sense to create a larger living space from two small rooms front and back. Many a home 'improver' had little respect for architectural details from an earlier age. What was the point of them?

Dado rails, picture rails and cornices were fussy adornments which could easily be ripped away; remove that ceiling boss and it was much easier to apply a coat of dimpled Artex; internal wooden doors could only be improved by a few thick layers of bright paint; and elegant, tiled fireplaces were best sold off to an antiques dealer, the space boarded up with plywood behind a modern gas fire.

In their cheerful, freshly designed pads the young things of the Sixties enjoyed more home entertainment than any generation had ever known before, although they provided little of it themselves. There was no need for an old-fashioned knees-up with uncle punishing the ivories when so much professional music was available on your stereo record player, so much first-rate comedy and drama on your television set – a luxury owned by about two-thirds of the population at the beginning of the decade, but by nearly everyone at the end of it.

And what choice! Whether in the clubs, the discos, the cinemas, the theatres, the artists' studios or the writers' garrets, a burst of creativity in the arts and entertainment seemed to be making the world anew…

‘Rock and Roll: music for the neck downwards.’

Rolling Stone Keith Richards

Chapter four

SERGEANT PEPPER AND FRIENDS

Although the Sixties echoed to a great many sounds, the aural landscape was dominated by four Liverpool lads who, after rendering their female fans hysterical with raw numbers such as 'Love Me Do' and 'Please Please Me', developed an astonishing and unheralded musical range and subtlety before breaking up to go their separate ways.

The Beatles had their first UK success in 1962, stopped touring in 1966 and released their last album in 1970 – by which time they were millionaires several times over.

In one sense they were typical of the period. Most stars from the Fifties and before had been individuals performing other people's numbers, but the Sixties saw a mushrooming of groups who (for better or worse) wrote their own songs.

Elvis was still the King (though making a run of insipid films) and rock legends such as Roy Orbison and Chuck Berry were still going strong, but in the UK it was the groups – most of them British – who made the running.

The Dansette

The must-have piece of equipment for a rock-happy teenager in the Fifties and Sixties was a portable Dansette record player. Shaped like a small suitcase, but with a brightly coloured leatherette casing in red, blue, pink, green or cream, it was designed for discs played at any of three prevailing speeds: 33⅓, 45 and 78 rpm (revolutions per minute).

The 45 rpm 'single' allowed about three minutes' playing time on each side, the A-side being the hoped-for hit number, with the B-side, or flip-side, offering something more anodyne.

One vital ingredient in the Beatles' success was their manager, Brian Epstein, who in the early days of their relationship persuaded them to trim their hair and abandon their leather jackets and jeans for suits. He had, he said, been drawn to them not only by their music but by their sense of humour, too.

It seems a little strange in hindsight, but the four 'mopheads' were for a time regarded as the respectable kind of young lads you could take home to mother, compared with the raucous and overtly sexual Rolling Stones, led by the pouting, preening and androgynous Mick Jagger.

Production values

Paul McCartney later said that Epstein was the true 'fifth Beatle', while George Harrison joked in tribute that the group's MBEs stood for 'Mr Brian Epstein'. Weeks before he died of an accidental drug overdose in August 1967, they had released one of the strangest and most successful albums in pop history – *Sgt Pepper's Lonely Hearts Club Band* – and had another behind-the-scenes man to thank.

With a *little* help from my friends

Here, as a treat for nostalgic readers, is an alphabetical list of three dozen Sixties groups, British and American, with one memorable number each from their repertoires:

- **Amen Corner** (If Paradise Is) Half as Nice
- **The Animals** House of the Rising Sun
- **The Beach Boys** Good Vibrations
- **The Beatles** Yesterday
- **The Bee Gees** Massachusetts
- **Billy J. Kramer and the Dakotas** Little Children
- **Cream** I Feel Free
- **The Dave Clark Five** Glad All Over
- **The Doors** Light My Fire
- **Fleetwood Mac** Albatross
- **The Four Seasons** Big Girls Don't Cry
- **Gary Puckett and the Union Gap** Young Girl
- **Gerry and the Pacemakers** How Do You Do It?
- **The Grateful Dead** Truckin'
- **Herman's Hermits** I'm Into Something Good
- **The Hollies** The Air that I Breathe
- **The Kinks** You Really Got Me
- **Manfred Mann** Mighty Quinn

- **Martha and the Vandellas** Heat Wave
- **The Monkees** I'm a Believer
- **The Moody Blues** Go Now
- **The Mothers of Invention** Who Are the Brain Police?
- **Pink Floyd** See Emily Play
- **Procol Harum** A Whiter Shade of Pale
- **The Rolling Stones** It's All Over Now
- **The Searchers** Don't Throw Your Love Away
- **The Seekers** The Carnival is Over
- **The Small Faces** Lazy Sunday
- **Status Quo** Pictures of Matchstick Men
- **The Supremes** Where Did Our Love Go?
- **The Swinging Blue Jeans** Hippy Hippy Shake
- **The Temptations** You're My Everything
- **The Troggs** Wild Thing
- **The Who** My Generation
- **The Yardbirds** For Your Love
- **The Zombies** She's Not There

The *Sgt Pepper* album couldn't possibly have been recreated on tour, because it was heavy with the kind of sophisticated production techniques for which the arranger and composer George Martin was renowned.

For John Lennon's song 'Being for the Benefit of Mr Kite!', for example, the sound engineers collected recordings of fairground organs, cut them into strips, edited them in random order and created a long loop which was mixed in during the final production.

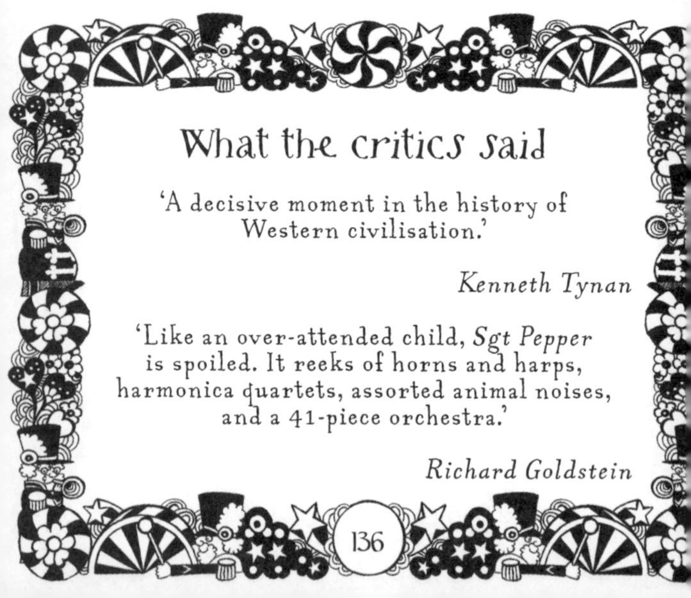

What the critics said

'A decisive moment in the history of Western civilisation.'

Kenneth Tynan

'Like an over-attended child, *Sgt Pepper* is spoiled. It reeks of horns and harps, harmonica quartets, assorted animal noises, and a 41-piece orchestra.'

Richard Goldstein

Martin had worked with the Beatles ever since they came under Epstein's wing, but this new record was altogether more extravagant than anything that had gone before. Gone was the idea of the musicians simply turning up for a few hours of banging out their individual songs and re-recording any sections that might have gone wrong. *Sgt Pepper* was put together over a period of 129 days, with orchestras and other musicians hired to replicate genres as varied as music-hall, rock and jazz, Western classical and traditional Indian music. It was, in short, a 'concept album'.

The brightly coloured cover (designed by pop artist Peter Blake and his then wife Jann Haworth), shows the Beatles dressed in extravagant military-style uniforms (designed by Manuel Cuevas) and standing behind a large drum (painted by the fairground artist Joe Ephgrave).

Behind them is a collage of more than 70 figures, most of them famous – and most of them men. Lennon was reportedly thwarted in an attempt to include Jesus Christ and Adolf Hitler, but the sitar-playing George Harrison successfully smuggled in a number of Indian gurus. The former Beatle Stuart Sutcliffe is there, and so is Bob Dylan. Freud, Jung, Marx and Einstein appear, as well as an array of writers, artists, comedians, actors and actresses (Shirley Temple's sweater carries the legend 'Welcome the Rolling Stones'). There are a few surprising inclusions:

- **Aleister Crowley (occultist)**
- **Sonny Liston (boxer)**
- **Sir Robert Peel (19th-century British prime minister)**
- **Karlheinz Stockhausen (avant-garde composer)**
- **Albert Stubbins (Liverpool footballer)**

Zapped by Frank

The Beatles never claimed to have produced the first concept album, but the fact that other people hyped it in this fashion seems to have annoyed Frank Zappa. His Mothers of Invention *could* lay claim to getting there first, and they had their revenge by guying the *Sgt Pepper* cover (the first of several such 'borrowings') for their next album, which they entitled *We're Only in It for the Money*.

Wild Nights at the Blue Boar

A humble all-night café serving traditional working-men's fare became a veritable honeypot for Sixties rock stars and their hangers-on.

This was the Blue Boar café (now the Watford Gap service station) on Britain's very first motorway, the M1.

Here, for the price of a cup of tea, a mug of Bovril, a bacon sandwich or a plate of egg and chips, you could mingle with the big names of the time on their way up and down the country between gigs.

Their beaten-up Transit vans were a regular feature of the Blue Boar car park, and for rockers with an American yearning (and that meant a great many of them) the M1 acquired some of the romanticism of the legendary Chicago–Los Angeles road, Route 66.

At a time when the country was still suffering from austerity, the very fact that you could call in at a greasy spoon at any time of the night was a luxury – and mingling with the likes of Pink Floyd, the Rolling Stones, the Moody Blues and Status Quo was an incredible bonus.

As the title suggests, something else was bugging Zappa. He was no friend of hippiedom, and he regarded the Beatles' latest venture – with its psychedelic cover and songs about drugs – as a crass commercialisation of a movement he despised. Rock and roll might have become more complex and interesting, but (in this case, at least) he thought it had lost its soul.

Electrifying performances

Hadn't we heard this kind of complaint before? Yes, as recently as 1966 – and this time the accused had been not the Beatles but Bob Dylan.

The impact of Dylan on the Sixties hardly needs rehearsing, and it was as powerful in the UK as in America. Here was the folksinger as prophet, protestor, social conscience. The declared influence was Woody Guthrie, who had chronicled the plight of itinerant 'dustbowl' families in the 1930s. Dylan's voice was rasping, the words poetic (the English critic Christopher Ricks famously included him in his pantheon), the tone uncompromising.

But if the times they were a-changin', so was Dylan himself. The burning issue wasn't his political stance (always enigmatically blurred in his mumbling public utterances) but something much more straightforward: he had begun playing an electric guitar.

The first murmurings of discontent were heard at the Newport Folk Festival on Rhode Island in 1965, where he performed with a rock band. The criticism intensified during his world tour the following year, and climaxed in his UK shows, during which he played acoustic guitar in the first half and switched to electric in the second.

At the Free Trade Hall in Manchester that May he was subjected to a yell of 'Judas!' In the Odeon Theatre, Liverpool, someone demanded to know where his conscience had gone, and he replied 'There's a guy up there looking for a saint.' At the Royal Albert Hall in London there were walk-outs during the last two nights of the tour, although he had some welcome support from the Beatles, who were in the audience and remonstrated with the hecklers, whom Harrison called 'idiots'.

Enduring Cliff

It may seem strange to mention him in this exalted company, but the evergreen Sir Cliff Richard helps us keep our bearings among the psychedelic swirl. His 1958 single 'Move It' has been described as Britain's first authentic rock and roll hit – John Lennon once said that 'Before Cliff and the Shadows, there had been nothing worth listening to in British music' – but his subsequent stream of middle-of-the-road chart successes reminds us that (as with other artistic and social changes during this turbulent decade) there were always steadier, more conservative currents below the surface.

Cliff was, and remains, a tuneful troubadour of an enduring kind, and the period's string of crooners and belters included the likes of Frank Sinatra, Dean Martin, Shirley Bassey, Engelbert Humperdinck, Tom Jones, Dusty Springfield, Frankie Vaughan, Cilla Black, Jim Reeves and Andy Williams.

Dare we also mention that 'Tears', by the toothy comedian Ken Dodd, was the best-selling disc of 1965?

On the glum side

Perhaps psychologists can explain it, but there was a curious penchant for 'teenage tragedy' songs during the Sixties. Here are just four:

Teen Angel (Mark Dinning, 1960)
When their car stalls on a railway track, the boy pulls his girl to safety. Alas, she returns to it and is hit by a train. In her hand is the ring he gave her – that's what she went back for.

Tell Laura I Love Her (Ray Peterson, 1960)
Tommy sends a message that he may be late. He's taking part in a stock-car race so he can raise the cash to marry Laura. He's killed.

Leader of the Pack (The Shangri-Las, 1964)
When mum and dad warn their daughter off the boss of the motorcycle gang, she tells him it's over – and he speeds away to his death.

Ode to Billie Joe (Bobbie Gentry, 1967)
Why, we can only guess, but Billie Joe McCallister has jumped off the Tallahatchie Bridge – and only the singer seems to care.

Beware pirates!

Young rock fans could play music on their Dansettes, and watch ITV's *Ready Steady Go* (1963–1966) and the BBC's *Top of the Pops* (1964–2006), but when they turned the knobs of their transistor radios beyond Radio Luxembourg they found their tastes poorly served by the only alternative, the BBC's Light Programme. This gap in the market was filled for a while by so-called 'pirate' radio stations, which set up their studios on boats moored just outside British territorial waters.

Blacking up

How times change! Back in the Sixties one of the most popular TV entertainments was the weekly *Black and White Minstrel Show*, in which white singers and dancers blacked up in order to enact over-the-top stereotypes of black performers. By 1964 it had a regular audience of more than 18 million viewers.

In May 1967 the Campaign Against Racial Discrimination delivered a petition to the BBC calling for its removal from the airwaves. Although briefly rested in 1969, the show soon returned and lasted until 1978.

The first pirate station was Radio Caroline, which anchored the former Danish ferry *Fredericia* 3 miles (5 km) off Felixstowe on the Suffolk coast. A few weeks later Radio Atlanta followed suit, its former coaster MV *Mi Amigo* positioned a little way off Harwich, Essex. The two soon merged, and others followed.

These operations were hugely enjoyable for their novice broadcasters, and they attracted a huge audience – as two of the first DJs soon found out.

• When Tony Blackburn was coming home on shore leave on one occasion, he told listeners that he would be bringing back some records, and that anyone who wanted one should wave him down in his distinctive red MG Sprite. 'It took me six hours to get to London,' he said. 'I kept having to stop to explain that I'd run out of records.'

• Johnnie Walker was a Radio Caroline DJ when it operated off Frinton in Essex. He had the idea of inviting listeners to drive to the coast one evening, park opposite the boat and flash their lights when he gave the word. 'It was the greatest moment of megalomania in my life,' he said. I stood up on deck and said "Lights on!" and the entire coastline was illuminated as far as the eye could see. That was the Frinton Flash.'

Needless to say, this uncontrolled commercialism was too much for the government to bear. In 1966 the postmaster general, Anthony Wedgwood Benn, introduced a bill to Parliament outlawing unlicensed offshore broadcasting, and the Marine Offences Act became law the following August.

Radio 1

Governments need to be popular if they're to be re-elected, and this one was swift to placate young voters and potential voters by creating an entirely new BBC radio station catering for their needs. Radio 1 was launched on 30 September 1967, when the Light Programme, the Third Programme and the Home Service were given the numbers, respectively, 2, 3 and 4.

Tony Blackburn hosted that very first programme, and this was his playlist:

- **Flowers in the Rain** The Move
- **Massachusetts** The Bee Gees
- **Even the Bad Times Are Good** The Tremeloes
- **Fakin' It** Simon & Garfunkel
- **The Day I Met Marie** Cliff Richard
- **You Can't Hurry Love** The Supremes
- **The Last Waltz** Engelbert Humperdinck
- **Baby, Now that I've Found You** The Foundations
- **Good Times** Eric Burdon and the Animals
- **A Banda** Herb Alpert & the Tijuana Brass
- **I Feel Love Comin' On** Felice Taylor
- **How Can I Be Sure?** Young Rascals
- **Major to Minor** The Settlers
- **Homburg** Procol Harum
- **You Keep Running Away** The Four Tops
- **Let's Go to San Francisco** The Flower Pot Men
- **Handy Man** Jimmy James
- **You Know What I Mean** The Turtles
- **The House that Jack Built** The Alan Price Set
- **Excerpt from a Teenage Opera** Keith West
- **Reflections** Diana Ross and the Supremes
- **King Midas in Reverse** The Hollies
- **Ode To Billie Joe** Bobbie Gentry
- **Then He Kissed Me** The Crystals
- **Anything Goes** Harpers Bizarre
- **The Letter** The Box Tops
- **Beefeaters** John Dankworth

Isle of Wight

For American hippies there was Woodstock, and for their British counterparts there was… the Isle of Wight. From 1968 to 1970 its August rock festival drew thousands on the ferry from the mainland.

The first event was relatively small: some 10,000 turned up to enjoy Jefferson Airplane, The Move, Arthur Brown, Pretty Things, Plastic Penny and Tyrannosaurus Rex.

Juke Box Jury

Its panel was a strange mixture of the young and (predominantly) middle-aged, but BBC TV's *Juke Box Jury*, compèred by David Jacobs, was a popular evening fixture every week until 1967. Four celebrities would decide whether each newly released recording was a Hit or a Miss, with an appropriate sound effect for each verdict.

By 1962 there was a regular audience of 12 million viewers, although this practically doubled on 7 December 1963 when the Beatles formed the panel.

By the following year word had got around. Now 150,000 flocked to the island, where there was a special attraction. Bob Dylan, who had injured himself in a motorbike accident not long after his bad experience at the Albert Hall (see page 141), was making his comeback appearance after an absence of almost three years. (What attracted him, apparently, was the thought of performing in Tennyson country, the Victorian poet having made his home on the island.)

In the audience for Dylan on the final night was a remarkable galaxy of rock stars – John Lennon (with Yoko Ono), Ringo Starr, George Harrison, Keith Richards, Bill Wyman, Syd Barrett, Eric Clapton and Elton John – plus the actress Jane Fonda.

The 1970 festival may be technically just beyond our period, but we ought to record that it notched up an attendance thought to be in excess of 600,000 to watch Jimi Hendrix, the Doors, the Who and Joan Baez, but that it ran into so many political and logistical difficulties that there wouldn't be another on the island for all of 32 years.

UK's best-selling singles of the Sixties

1960 **It's Now or Never** Elvis Presley
1961 **Are You Lonesome Tonight?** Elvis Presley
1962 **I Remember You** Frank Ifield
1963 **She Loves You** The Beatles
1964 **Can't Buy Me Love** The Beatles
1965 **Tears** Ken Dodd
1966 **Green, Green Grass of Home** Tom Jones
1967 **Release Me** Engelbert Humperdinck
1968 **Hey, Jude** The Beatles
1969 **Sugar, Sugar** The Archies

UK's best-selling albums of the Sixties

1960 **South Pacific** soundtrack
1961 **G.I. Blues** Elvis Presley
1962 **West Side Story** soundtrack
1963 **With the Beatles** The Beatles
1964 **Beatles for Sale** The Beatles
1965 **The Sound of Music** soundtrack
1966 **The Sound of Music** soundtrack
1967 **Sgt Pepper's Lonely Hearts Club Band** The Beatles
1968 **The Sound of Music** soundtrack
1969 **Abbey Road** The Beatles

Upbeat verse

Poets don't usually attract the razzmatazz of a rock concert, but the grandly named International Poetry Incarnation at the Albert Hall in June 1965 for a brief moment promoted 'beat' culture to centre-stage.

Its leading figure was the bearded, bearlike Allen Ginsberg (see page 17), who had arrived in London the previous month offering to read anywhere for free and who declaimed his verse, sang to finger-cymbals and was enthusiastically pelted with flowers. With him were two fellow American poets, Gregory Corso and Lawrence Ferlinghetti, and a host of others, chiefly British.

The flavour of the evening's wilder reaches can be gauged from a paragraph in the official programme:

World declaration hot peace shower! Earth's grass is free! Cosmic poetry Visitation accidental happening carnally! Spontaneous planet-chant Carnival! Mental Cosmonaut poet epiphany, immaculate supranational Poesy insemination!

Some 7,000 people witnessed this free-wheeling four-hour 'happening' – far and away the largest-ever audience for a UK poetry reading – and more were turned away at the doors. The verse they heard was uneven in quality (the performers were sometimes heckled as well as applauded) and in approach (ranging from the personal to the political).

Corso, for instance, read a long and difficult poem that probably needed to be first seen on the page, whereas the English poet Adrian Mitchell memorably declaimed his poem 'To Whom It May Concern', with its stark and immediately accessible anti-war message:

> I was run over by the truth one day.
> Ever since the accident I've walked this way
> So stick my legs in plaster
> Tell me lies about Vietnam.

The *Times Literary Supplement* commented that the event had 'made literary history by a combination of flair, courage, and seized opportunities'. Jeff Nuttall, whose 1968 book *Bomb Culture* chronicled the emergence of internationalist counter-culture in Britain, later wrote that 'The Underground was suddenly there on the surface.' Christopher Logue, who himself performed at the Albert Hall, reflected that 'Time makes short work of bad verse. Literary standards were not high that day. It did not matter. It was the moment that spoke.'

Some poetry published in the Sixties

- **Summoned by Bells** John Betjeman
- **My Sad Captains** Thom Gunn
- **Wodwo** Ted Hughes
- **King Log** Geoffrey Hill
- **The Whitsun Weddings** Philip Larkin
- **Summer with Monika** Roger McGough
- **Notes to the Hurrying Man** Brian Patten
- **Ariel** Sylvia Plath
- **The Bread of Truth** R. S. Thomas

A trio of London theatres

- Established by the actor Bernard Miles at Puddle Dock, Blackfriars, in 1959, the **Mermaid Theatre** was the first built in the City of London since Shakespeare's day. It was a thriving venue in the Sixties, with a stage thrust out into the audience on three sides.

- Whereas the Mermaid later declined and closed, the **Donmar Warehouse** at Covent Garden has grown in importance since Donald Albery first converted it into a private drama studio and rehearsal room for Margot Fonteyn's Royal Festival Ballet in 1961. ('Donmar' comes from the first syllables of their Christian names.)

  The Royal Shakespeare Company bought it as a theatre in 1977 and put on productions there until 1990, when Roger Wingate took it over and completely rebuilt it.

- In 1964 the prolific playwright Arnold Wesker converted a listed former railway engine shed at Chalk Farm into **The Roundhouse** – a venue for his Centre 42 Theatre Company. Today it specialises in live music, and in 2010 it set up its own in-house record label, Roundhouse Records.

Marat/Sade

A comparable moment in Sixties theatre was the electrifying London production in 1964 of Peter Weiss's *Marat/Sade* – or, to give the full title, *The Persecution and Assassination of Jean-Paul Marat as Performed by the Inmates of the Asylum of Charenton under the Direction of the Marquis de Sade*. (Adrian Mitchell wrote the screenplay for a 1967 film version.)

The work had first been performed in West Berlin earlier that year, but it was Peter Brook's staging in an English translation which won it acclaim – and some notoriety. The play is set in the bath hall of a lunatic asylum during the French Revolution, and its rawness and brutality (de Sade is whipped, for example) shocked and offended some who came to see it. Fractured in style and interspersed with music, it deals in part with the plight of the downtrodden, a recurrent chorus being:

Marat, we're poor and the poor stay poor,
Marat, don't make us wait any more.
We want our rights and we don't care how,
We want our revolution NOW.

'Most audiences experienced it as powerful,' found the critic David Richard Jones. 'Viewers showed that they were strongly affected by its magnitude, whether they walked out in anger or stayed seated, shaking, at the end. . . . At least one spectator, the German actress Ruth Arrack, died in the auditorium during a performance.'

Some Sixties plays

- **The Caretaker** Harold Pinter
- **A Man for All Seasons** Robert Bolt
- **Luther** John Osborne
- **Chips With Everything** Arnold Wesker
- **Entertaining Mr Sloane** Joe Orton
- **The Royal Hunt of the Sun** Peter Shaffer
- **The Homecoming** Harold Pinter
- **A Patriot for Me** John Osborne
- **Relatively Speaking** Alan Ayckbourn
- **Saved** Edward Bond
- **Loot** Joe Orton
- **Inadmissible Evidence** John Osborne
- **A Day in the Death of Joe Egg** Peter Nichols
- **Forty Years On** Alan Bennett
- **Rosencrantz and Guildenstern Are Dead** Tom Stoppard
- **What the Butler Saw** Joe Orton
- **Oh! Calcutta!** Kenneth Tynan

Shock and awe

Though Joe Orton would probably have regretted a death in his audience, there was nothing he liked better than causing shock and offence. His first act was criminal (he and his lover, Kenneth Halliwell, were jailed in 1962 for stealing art books from libraries and defacing others with filthily humorous additions), and his last act was tragic (in 1967 Halliwell bludgeoned him to death with a hammer). Between those two events he wrote a series of wickedly nonconformist black comedies rich in vigorous dialogue and Wildean conceits.

It was Edward Bond, however, who provided the sharpest goad for the Lord Chancellor before censorship was abolished in 1968. His play *Saved* included a scene in which a baby was stoned to death in its pram – and its banning proved a *cause célèbre*. Since the work dealt with the causes of violence among the economically depressed south London working class, Bond insisted the scene was an essential part of the action, and he refused to remove it.

The Royal Court Theatre and its artistic director Wlliam Gaskill thought they had found a way of blunting the blue pencil by turning their venue into a club theatre under the aegis of the English Stage Society, and they gave a first performance of *Saved* on 3 November 1965. It was a ploy which didn't work: the Society was prosecuted – not for the violence itself, but for performing an unlicensed play.

Many critics had deplored Bond's subject matter in general as well as the baby-stoning in particular, although Philip Hope-Wallace in the *Guardian* pointed out that the scene was no more horrible than parts of Shakespeare's *Titus Adronicus*, and Laurence Olivier (then artistic director of the National Theatre) defended the play as being 'for grown-ups, and the grown-ups of this country should have the courage to look at it'.

The Stage Society lost its case but was given a conditional discharge, and *Saved*, which immediately became a huge success around the world, proved to be the last play to be prosecuted in Britain.

Bond's next work, the surreal *Early Morning*, would certainly have met the same fate had the tide not already been turning. This included a lesbian relationship between Queen Victoria and Florence Nightingale, portrayed the royal princes as what were then known as Siamese twins, and had Disraeli and Prince Albert plotting a coup before everyone fell off Beachy Head. The Royal Court defied a ban to produce it, but no prosecution was forthcoming, and within a year the law had been repealed.

Last exit for the DPP

The *Lady Chatterley's Lover* furore (see pages 23–26) might have appeared to ring-fence serious fiction from prosecution, but there was to be one last stand by those who wished to drive obscenity underground. This time the flak was aimed at an overseas import: *Last Exit to Brooklyn* by the American author Hubert Selby, Jr.

After it was published in the UK by Calder and Boyars in 1966, the Director of Public Prosecutions (DPP) declined to take any action, but the Tory MP for Wimbledon, Sir Cyril Black, was so incensed by its content that he initiated a successful private action before Marlborough Street magistrates' court in Soho, the witnesses for the prosecution including the publishers Sir Basil Blackwell and Robert Maxwell.

Ronnie Scott's

The centre of the British jazz universe in the Sixties was Ronnie Scott's club in London, which opened in Gerrard Street late in 1959 and moved to nearby Frith Street in Soho six years later.

Scott was a tenor saxophonist, who earned rare praise from the great Charles Mingus: 'Of the white boys, Ronnie Scott gets closer to the negro blues feeling.'

He founded the club with fellow sax player Pete King, and was the regular MC there, introducing the often stellar performers with a stream of jokes and one-liners.

Since the restriction on the book's sale applied only to the immediate Soho area, John Calder announced that he would be selling it everywhere else – a stance which prompted the DPP to prefer criminal charges.

In an echo of the Mervyn Griffith-Jones comment about wives and servants, Judge Graham Rigers decided that the case should be heard by an entirely male jury, as women 'might be embarrassed at having to read a book which dealt with homosexuality, prostitution, drug-taking and sexual perversion'.

A guilty verdict was returned, but in 1968 the lawyer and writer John Mortimer appealed against it, and a judgement by Mr Justice Lane reversed the ruling – so marking a seemingly irreversible shift in the obscenity laws in regard to literature. By that time more than half a million paperback copies had already been sold in the United States – read, one imagines, by women as often as men.

Some British novels of the Sixties

1960
A Burnt-Out Case Graham Greene
Clea Lawrence Durrell
A Kind of Loving Stan Barstow
The L-Shaped Room Lynne Reid Banks
Take a Girl Like You Kingsley Amis

1961
The Old Men at the Zoo Angus Wilson
The Prime of Miss Jean Brodie Muriel Spark
A Severed Head Iris Murdoch

1962
A Clockwork Orange Anthony Burgess
Down There on a Visit Christopher Isherwood
Life at the Top John Braine

1963
The Collector John Fowles
Inside Mr Enderby Anthony Burgess
Up the Junction Nell Dunn

1964
Corridors of Power C. P. Snow
Nothing Like the Sun Anthony Burgess
The Spire William Golding

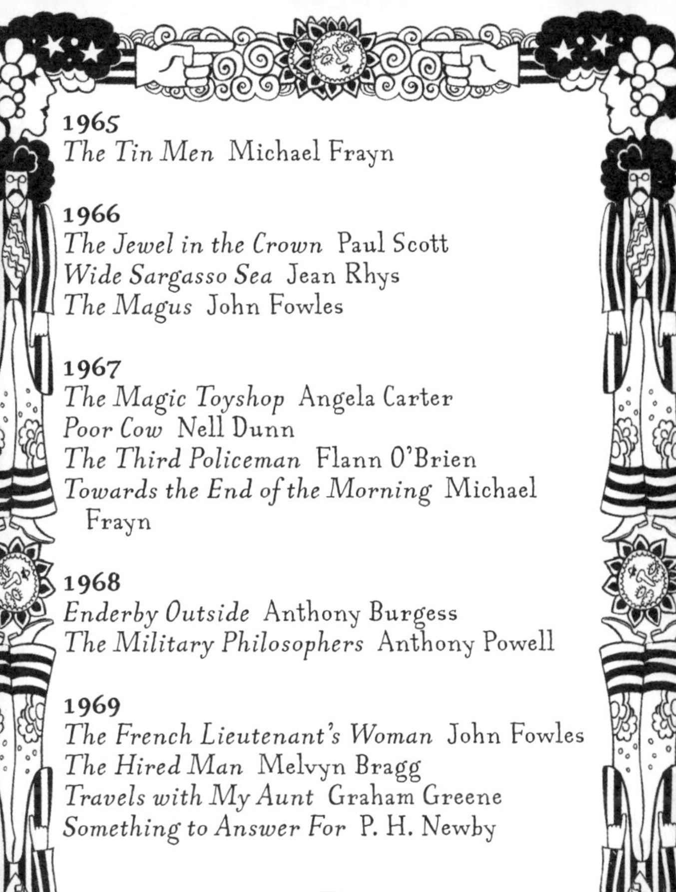

1965

The Tin Men Michael Frayn

1966

The Jewel in the Crown Paul Scott
Wide Sargasso Sea Jean Rhys
The Magus John Fowles

1967

The Magic Toyshop Angela Carter
Poor Cow Nell Dunn
The Third Policeman Flann O'Brien
Towards the End of the Morning Michael Frayn

1968

Enderby Outside Anthony Burgess
The Military Philosophers Anthony Powell

1969

The French Lieutenant's Woman John Fowles
The Hired Man Melvyn Bragg
Travels with My Aunt Graham Greene
Something to Answer For P. H. Newby

The two cultures

It was at the very end of the previous decade that the physicist C. P. Snow had delivered his *Two Cultures* lecture at Cambridge, but his argument that the liberal arts and the sciences were disciplines which operated in mutual ignorance reverberated through the Sixties. That was partly because the literary critic F. R. Leavis launched a vitriolic attack on Snow in a 1962 Cambridge lecture of his own – 'Not only is he not a genius; he is intellectually as undistinguished as it is possible to be' – and partly because Harold Wilson's 'white heat of technology' had given science and technology something of a shot in the arm.

It was also because Snow kept the pot boiling through his eleven-part novel sequence, *Strangers and Brothers*, set in the intense, back-stabbing worlds of academia and politics. The author's 'realism' is often synonymous with tedium (Leavis's literary appraisal was justly wounding), but at least a serious issue got a thorough public airing.

Queasy designs

The darling of the Sixties abstractionist Op-Art movement was Bridget Riley, her black-and-white geometrical designs producing such a sense of movement that some viewers reported feelings akin to seasickness.

She began 'investigating' colour in 1967. The following year she became the first British contemporary artist, and the first woman, to be awarded the International Prize for Painting at the Venice Biennale.

Edible art

There was plenty of aggro, too, in an art world seething with new theories and techniques. The sculptor Anthony Caro rejected the figurative bronzes of Henry Moore in favour of colour and abstraction (shapes in plastic and sheet metal laid out on the floor), and this in turn brought a reaction from conceptual artists such as John Latham.

Performance art was all the rage, and in 1966 Latham took part in the Destruction in Art symposium – an international gathering of artists, poets and scientists – by constructing three piles of books outside the British Museum and setting fire to them. Unfortunately the authorities were more concerned with health and safety than artistic expression, and the police and fire brigade swiftly brought the 'happening' to a close.

Latham was a part-time lecturer at Saint Martin's School of Art, and he demonstrated his disapproval of Clement Greenberg's cult book *Art and Culture* by borrowing a copy from the college's library and inviting students to eat it. The pulp from the chewed pages was distilled into a clear juice over the course of several months, and Latham eventually returned this concoction to the library instead of the book. He lost his job, but the phial of liquid and the correspondence about it are now on display at the Museum of Modern Art in New York.

It was in this iconoclastic atmosphere that the young Gilbert and George first made their mark, an early 'work' being their offering to fellow art students of baked beans in ice-cream cones.

fifteen minutes of fame

It was in an exhibition catalogue in Stockholm in 1968 that the American Pop artist Andy Warhol first made the comment that has been repeated *ad nauseam* ever since: 'In the future everyone will be world-famous for 15 minutes.'

Warhol himself, of course, managed a more lasting fame as a painter, film-maker, record producer and author, and he made a fortune from it: the highest price paid for one of his paintings was US$100 million for the 1963 canvas *Eight Elvises*.

You can visit the Andy Warhol Museum in his home town of Pittsburgh, Pennsylvania.

A sextet of sixties composers

- **Benjamin Britten** War Requiem, 1962
- **Michael Tippett** King Priam (opera), 1962
- **John Tavener** The Whale (dramatic cantata), 1966
- **Alexander Goehr** Arden Must Die (opera), 1966
- **Harrison Birtwhistle** Punch and Judy (opera), 1968
- **Peter Maxwell Davies** Eight Songs for a Mad King (monodrama), 1969

Pop goes the easel

Pop art originated in the Fifties, but it was at the 1961 Young Contemporaries exhibition at the RBA Galleries in London that Peter Blake and David Hockney effectively launched the British Pop Art movement.

Hockney was in part influenced by the expressionism of Francis Bacon, whose work was still a force in Sixties art, but the chief preoccupation of Pop art was using images from popular culture, including commercial logos and labels (Warhol's soup cans) and characters from comic books. Hockney would later spend years in California (the location of his famous swimming-pool scenes) before returning to his native Yorkshire, where his prolific output includes portraits, still lifes and landscapes.

Blake strayed less far, both from home and from his Pop art roots. How fitting that in 2009 he should potter around London in a double-decker bus painted with many of his familiar images, before taking it on a day trip to a contemporary cultural hotspot, Brighton. Blake brings our chapter full circle – as the designer of the *Sgt Pepper* album cover and as a Pop artist who fused high and low culture to such a degree that you'd find it hard to slide a paintbrush bristle between them.

The Sixties encouraged a spirit of adventurous eclecticism in the arts and entertainment, and there was much more on offer at the end of the decade than there had been at the beginning.

Some audiences were, of course, distinct, but many of the newly well-off 'consumers' found nothing strange in visiting a concert hall one evening and sitting down to enjoy *Steptoe and Son* on television the next; coming home from the latest James Bond film to grapple with a serious novel; or taking in a visit to an art gallery before setting off to sleep under damp canvas at a rock concert.

For the optimistic and enthusiastic this felt like a brave new world – and one that would never end.

Sixties TV sitcoms

with dates of first showing

- Marriage Lines 1961
- The Rag Trade 1961
- Steptoe and Son 1962
- The Likely Lads 1964
- Till Death Us Do Part 1966
- Dad's Army 1968
- The Liver Birds 1969

Most watched programmes

(with viewing figures in millions)

1 World Cup Final 1966 (32.3)
2 The Royal Family 1969 (30.69)
3 Royal Variety Performance 1965 (24.2)
4 News: Kennedy assassination 1963 (24.15)
5 Miss World 1967 (23.76)
6 Apollo 8 splashdown 1967 (22.55)
7 London Palladium Show 1967 (21.89)
8 Steptoe and Son 1964 (21.54)
9 Coronation Street 1964 (21.36)
10 Mrs Thursday 1966 (21.01)
11 Secombe and Friends 1966 (20.79)
12 Churchill's funeral 1965 (20.06)

A dozen Sixties cinema hits

- **Psycho** 1960
- **The Hustler** 1961
- **The Manchurian Candidate** 1962
- **Lawrence of Arabia** 1962
- **Dr No** 1962
- **From Russia With Love** 1963
- **Dr Strangelove** 1964
- **The War Game** 1965
- **The Good, the Bad and the Ugly** 1966
- **Cool Hand Luke** 1967
- **2001: A Space Odyssey** 1968
- **Butch Cassidy and the Sundance Kid** 1969

A dozen arthouse films

- **La Dolce Vita** Federico Fellini, 1960
- **Breathless** Jean-Luc Godard, 1960
- **L'Avventura** Michelangelo Antonioni, 1960
- **Viridiana** Luis Buñuel, 1961
- **Last Year at Marienbad** Alain Resnais, 1961
- **Yojimbo** Akira Kurosawa, 1961
- **Jules et Jim** François Truffaut, 1962
- **The Leopard** Luchino Visconti, 1963
- **8½** Federico Fellini, 1963
- **Blow-Up** Michelangelo Antonioni, 1966
- **Persona** Ingmar Bergman, 1966
- **Belle de Jour** Luis Buñuel, 1967

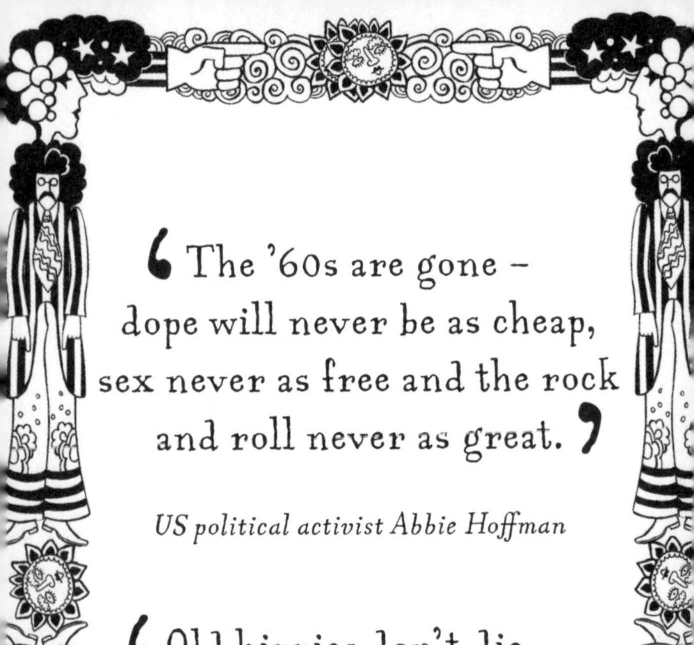

“The ’60s are gone –
dope will never be as cheap,
sex never as free and the rock
and roll never as great.”

US political activist Abbie Hoffman

“Old hippies don’t die –
they just lie low until the
laughter stops and their time
comes round again.”

British novelist Joseph Gallivan

CHAPTER *five*

TALKING 'BOUT MY GENERATION

It was such a very long time ago, and yet for many who experienced it the glory that was the Sixties lingers on like a dim but steady harbour light glimpsed through a pall of fog.

At the individual level the decade bequeathed a generation the hope of perpetual renewal, its ancients approaching their threescore years and ten in the unshakable belief that they had somehow bypassed the dreaded languors of slow-motion, pipe-and-slippers middle age altogether. 'Hope I die before I get old,' the Who had chorused – and the ideal solution was not to get old at all.

Sure enough, an improbable gaggle of Sixties rockers can still be seen performing their up-tempo, sexually charged music at bus-pass age. Paul McCartney, who had once regarded 64 as the gateway to decrepitude ('Will you still need me, will you still feed me?'), was not only composing, singing and recording at 69, but marrying for the third time, too.

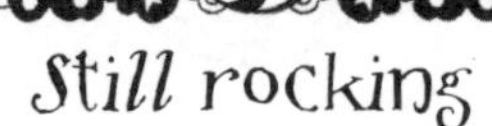

- Chuck Berry (born 1926)
- Jerry Lee Lewis (1935)
- Cliff Richard (1940)
- Bob Dylan (1941)
- Paul McCartney (1942)
- Gerry Marsden (1942)
- Ray Davies (1944)
- Van Morrison (1945)
- Wayne Fontana (1945)

The Rolling Stones:
- Charlie Watts (1941)
- Mick Jagger (1943)
- Keith Richards (1943)
- Ronnie Woods (1947)

The Who:
- Roger Daltry (1944)
- Pete Townshend (1945)

At the broader, social level the legacy of the Sixties is more problematic. Certainly the rebel leaders of the time were prone to displays of embarrassing self-indulgence:

- The newly married John Lennon and Yoko Ono invited the media to photograph them in bed every day for a week in the honeymoon suite at the Amsterdam Hilton Hotel in March 1969 – a stunt intended to promote world peace.
- Bob Dylan, apparently high on cannabis, laughed his way through the 1966 recording of 'Rainy Day Women #12 & 35', with the lyric 'Everybody must get stoned.'
- The leaders of the student uprising in Paris in 1968 brilliantly condemned the excesses of the West's industrial-military complex, but found nothing to offer in their place but slogans such as 'Be realistic – ask for the impossible' and 'Take your desires for realities.'

The UK reality was that the liberal spirit of the time took root in legislation introduced by men in suits (Harold Wilson's Labour government, that is) rather than through the sit-ins, protest songs and 'happenings' of the idealistic young. Dreams, as they quickly discovered, would never be enough.

So how much of that spirit survived the decade? Certainly those heady idealists would be given plenty to shake their heads about in the years ahead. Here are just four body blows among many:

Exhibit A: The Kissinger peace prize
When the US diplomat Henry Kissinger won the Nobel peace prize in 1973, the singer-songwriter Tom Lehrer commented mordantly that political satire had become obsolete. Kissinger was given the award for negotiating the end of the Vietnam war, but nobody on the left forgot his role as an exponent of cynical realpolitik while serving as secretary of state under Richard Nixon. The 'enemy' had been rewarded.

Exhibit B: No such thing as society
In 1987 the British prime minister Margaret Thatcher (in office 1979–1990) gave an interview to *Woman's Own* magazine in which she made a comment that defined her political philosophy:

'I think we have gone through a period when too many children and people have been given to understand "I have a problem, it is the government's job to cope with it!" "I am homeless, the government must house me!" And so they're casting their problems on society, and who is society? There is no such thing! There are individual men and women and there are families, and no government can do anything except through people, and people look to themselves first.'

There had been plenty of individualism in the Sixties, too, but there had also been a keen sense of shared interests – and by the Eighties that social cohesion seemed increasingly under threat.

Exhibit C: Blair's blame game

In 2004 the cadet Thatcherite and (Labour) prime minister Tony Blair took a fresh swing at the Sixties, blaming it for crime and family breakdown in his own time.

'A society of different lifestyles,' he claimed, 'spawned a group of young people who were brought up without parental discipline, without proper role models and without any sense of responsibility to others.

'Today people have had enough of this part of the 1960s consensus. People do not want a return to old prejudices and ugly discrimination, but they do want rules, order and proper behaviour. They want a community where the decent law-abiding majority are in charge.'

Ah, those feckless young people and that 'decent law-abiding majority'! It sounded such a throwback to the fusty old 1950s that the sclerotic sinews of the Sixties generation surely flexed in unison, ready to enter the fray all over again.

Exhibit D: God save the Queen

And whatever happened to the end of deference? With all those people scuttling from their cinema seats to avoid having to stand for the national anthem, surely the end of the monarchy was in sight?

Not a chance. This book is published in Elizabeth's diamond jubilee year, with opinion polls revealing that 70 per cent of the population opposes dropping the Crown in favour of a republic.

Ten films set in the Sixties

- **American Graffiti** California high-school friends spend a last summer of freedom before going to college.
- **Dirty Dancing** A romance in which Frances ('Baby') joins her family at a holiday camp and falls in love with the dancing teacher.
- **Easy Rider** Two counterculture bikers travel from LA to New Orleans to discover America.
- **Good Morning, Vietnam** A zany DJ shakes up the US Armed Services Radio station in Vietnam.
- **Hair** Adaptation of the 1968 musical in which a Vietnam war draftee goes hippie.
- **National Lampoon's Animal House** Comedy in which misfit fraternity members take on their university administration.
- **Taking Woodstock** Based on a true story about the 1969 festival.
- **The Day of the Jackal** A professional assassin plots to kill President Charles de Gaulle. Based on Frederick Forsyth's thriller.
- **The Deer Hunter** The Vietnam war affects the lives of people in a small American town.
- **Thirteen Days** Docudrama about the Cuban Missile Crisis of 1962.

PCGM

But all has not been lost. When Blair said he wanted no return of the 'old prejudices and ugly discrimination' he was conceding one of the abiding benefactions of the Sixties: a more relaxed society in which women have more control over their own bodies; unhappy couples are able to divorce without blame; racial minorities are protected from abuse; homosexuals are unmolested by the law; and the censor has dropped his blue pencil and gone into a welcome retirement.

Today, an over-zealous application of these principles is routinely described by conservative critics as 'political correctness', or 'PC' – often ratcheted up to 'political correctness gone mad'. The PCGM tag is applied with such a curl of the lip that it's clear the speaker would, if he could, do away with the relevant legislation altogether.

He can't, though. The Sixties have changed things, and changed them for the better.

Researching and writing this book has been almost a guilty pleasure, as if I were entrusted with a bottle of some precious liquid, the merest sniff at its every uncorking conjuring up a flood of pungent memories and images – private scenes, of course, but public events, too.

We are all, no doubt, prone to romanticise our formative years if we had the luck to be happy in them, but please allow me the conceit that the Sixties were, indeed, a little different and rather special. If it were in my power to grant it, I would wish just such an invigorating ambience of hope, self-expression and individual liberty on any youngster about to set out on the tremulous teenage adventure.

The Sixties? Yes, I *was* there, and I *do* remember them.

Glossary

10 Downing Street The official home of the British prime minister.

apartheid The system of racial discrimination practised in South Africa between 1948 and 1994.

Art Deco A decorative style featuring bold colours and geometric designs, popular in the 1920s and 30s.

Artex A trademark name for a textured ceiling material.

Art Nouveau A decorative style of c.1900 featuring flowing organic designs.

baby-boomer A member of the generation born in the immediate aftermath of the Second World War.

CND The Campaign for Nuclear Disarmament.

existentialism A system of philosophy stressing individual freedom and responsibility.

Fleet Street The British newspaper industry (formerly based in this London street).

GI An American soldier.

LSD Lysergic acid diethylamide, a powerful hallucinogenic drug.

Op Art A style of art which explores visual responses to patterns, often creating optical illusions.

Palais A once-popular name for a cinema.

prefab A factory-made, one-storey home assembled on site in reponse to the postwar housing shortage.

Scotland Yard The former headquarters of the Metropolitan Police.

Troubles, the The thirty years of sectarian violence in Northern Ireland, starting in the late Sixties.

white paper An official report outlining a proposed new government policy.

A Sixties timeline

1960

January End of Mau Mau uprising in Kenya.

February Prime Minister Harold Macmillan's 'Wind of Change' speech.

August First performance of satirical stage revue *Beyond the Fringe*.

September Betting and Gaming Act legalises betting shops.

November *Lady Chatterley* trial ends.

December First episode of soap opera *Coronation Street* on ITV. National conscription ends.

1961

August Berlin Wall divides the city.

September More than 1,300 arrested at CND rally in Trafalgar Square, London.

October Launch of satirical magazine *Private Eye*.

December Birth-control pills made available on the National Health Service.

1962

February *Sunday Times* publishes first colour supplement.

June Beatles play their first session at Abbey Road studios.

July Rolling Stones make their debut at the Marquee Club in London. Macmillan sacks a third of his cabinet in the 'Night of the Long Knives'.

September First broadcast of TV quiz show *University Challenge*.

October John Vassall jailed for spying. Cuban Missile Crisis.

November Launch of satirical TV revue *That Was The Week That Was.*

December Crick, Wilkins and Watson win Nobel Prize for their work on DNA.

1963

January Double agent Kim Philby defects to the USSR.

March Beatles' first LP, *Please Please Me*. Beeching Report recommends extensive rail closures.

April Nuclear weapons protesters march from Aldermaston to London.

June War minister John Profumo resigns over the Christine Keeler affair.

August The Great Train Robbery.

September Robbins Report recommends expansion of universities.

October Harold Macmillan resigns; Sir Alec Douglas-Home becomes prime minister.

November Dartford Tunnel (a road tunnel under the Thames east of London) opens. Assassination of US President John F. Kennedy.

1964

January Launch of *Jackie* magazine.

March Radio Caroline begins broadcasting. Mods and Rockers fight at Clacton.

April Launch of BBC 2 television.

May Terence Conran opens first Habitat store. Mods and Rockers fight at Brighton.

August First *Match of the Day* on BBC TV.
September Final edition of the *Daily Herald* and first edition of the *Sun*.
October Harold Wilson wins general election for Labour.

1965
January State funeral of Sir Winston Churchill.
July Great Train Robber Ronald Biggs escapes from Wandsworth prison.
August Cigarette advertising banned on TV. Documentary *The War Game* (depicting a nuclear strike on Britain) pulled from TV schedules for political reasons.
October Ian Brady and Myra Hindley charged with the sadistic Moors murders.
November Kenneth Tynan uses the F-word on British TV. Rhodesian government declares independence from the UK. Death penalty for murder abolished for five years.
December Race Relations Act.

1966
January Britain stops trade with Rhodesia.
March Labour wins increased majority at general election.
April *Time* magazine praises 'swinging London'.
June Barclays Bank introduces the first British credit card.
July Violent anti-Vietnam War protests in London. Ban on black workers at Euston Station is overturned. England wins the World Cup.

October Aberfan disaster: 144 people, including 116 children, are killed by a collapsing spoil tip in South Wales. Spy George Blake escapes from prison and travels to Moscow.

November Broadcast of drama-documentary *Cathy Come Home*.

1967

February British National Front founded.

May UK and Ireland apply to join the EEC.

June The Beatles release *Sgt Pepper* album. Rolling Stones Mick Jagger and Keith Richards jailed for drug possession. 'Summer of Love' in California.

July First colour TV broadcasts in UK. Sexual Offences Act decriminalises homosexual acts between consenting adults. British steel industry nationalised.

September Launch of the liner *QE2* and of Radio 1.

October Abortion Act. St Pancras station given Grade I listing. Che Guevara killed.

1968

January Beginning of the Prague Spring. 'I'm Backing Britain' campaign launched. Ford Escort introduced.

March Hundreds arrested at anti-Vietnam War protest in Grosvenor Square.

April US civil rights activist Martin Luther King assassinated. Enoch Powell MP makes 'Rivers of Blood' speech.

May Protest sit-ins at UK universities.

June US Senator Robert Kennedy assassinated.

July *Dad's Army* sitcom first broadcast.

August Britain's last mainline steam railway service runs from London to Carlisle.

September Theatres Act ends censorship. Musical *Hair* opens in London.

October Beginning of the 'Troubles' in Northern Ireland. Anti-Vietnam protests outside the US embassy in London.

November Race Relations Act passed.

1969

January Rupert Murdoch buys the *News of the World*. Student riots close London School of Economics.

March Maiden flight of Concorde. Kray twins convicted of murder. Opening of London underground's Victoria Line.

May Open University established.

June Divorce Reform Act establishes no-fault divorce.

July First Moon landing.

August British troops deployed in Northern Ireland to restore law and order.

October First episode of *Monty Python's Flying Circus*.

November Regular colour broadcasts begin on BBC and ITV.

December Death penalty permanently abolished for murder.

Index

E

F

G

H

I

J

K

L

M

N

O

P

Q

R

David Arscott was a newspaper journalist when the Sixties were 'happening'. He compares writing about them all these years later to feasting on a bumper tin of Proust's madeleines.